REMOTE WORK

Thrive in the New Age of Remote
and Hybrid Careers

S Nikolson

Kindle

INTRODUCTION

The work landscape has undergone a profound transformation in recent years, marking a seismic shift in how we approach our careers and daily responsibilities. The rise of remote and hybrid work models is not merely a passing trend but a revolution that fundamentally challenges the traditional notion of work. Today, professionals are no longer confined to the four walls of a physical office. Instead, the workplace has expanded, allowing for unprecedented flexibility and adaptability in ways we could only dream of a decade ago.

Remote work is now a permanent fixture in the modern professional world. The benefits of working from home are becoming increasingly apparent: reduced commuting times, increased autonomy over one's work environment, and the ability to create a personalized workspace tailored to individual preferences. The convenience of managing personal responsibilities alongside professional duties has transformed how individuals perceive work. With many people prioritizing their well-being, the flexibility to design a workday that accommodates both personal and professional commitments has become highly desirable. This shift has empowered employees to tailor their work-life balance and has fostered broader acceptance of diverse work arrangements, creating a more inclusive approach to employment.

Employers, too, are beginning to realize the advantages of flexible work arrangements. Companies that embrace remote work often discover that their employees are more satisfied, engaged, and productive when they feel trusted to manage their schedules. In this new paradigm, organizational success hinges on the ability to adapt to the evolving needs of the workforce. How well companies respond to these needs significantly influences employee engagement and loyalty. This emphasis on results over hours spent in the office has prompted a reevaluation of performance metrics, focusing on outcomes rather than activities.

As remote work becomes the norm, organizations focus on performance metrics reflecting this new reality. This requires a fundamental change in how productivity is measured and rewarded. Companies that successfully navigate this transition will be better positioned for long-term success. Adapting performance evaluations to reflect the unique challenges of remote work is crucial for fostering a culture of accountability and excellence.

Organizations must now look beyond traditional metrics and embrace innovative ways to assess employee contributions. For example, rather than solely evaluating based on hours logged or physical presence in the office, companies are starting to measure success through project completions, team collaborations, and customer satisfaction ratings. This shift aligns performance metrics with actual job responsibilities. It empowers employees to take ownership of their work, knowing that their contributions are valued based on results rather than mere presence.

As we embrace this new work era, we must consider how organizations adapt their physical spaces. Many are downsizing their office footprints, opting for co-working arrangements or hybrid models that allow employees to choose when they come into the office. For instance, Slack has boldly adopted a "digital-first" approach, reducing its physical office space while continuing to foster collaboration among its teams. This evolution illustrates that the traditional boundaries of work are dissolving, paving the way for a more fluid and dynamic approach to our professional lives.

Additionally, companies are beginning to understand that the design of their workspaces plays a crucial role in employee satisfaction and productivity. Open-concept offices, which were once all the rage, are being re-evaluated in favor of more flexible layouts that accommodate a variety of working styles. Companies are investing in technology that supports collaboration and communication, ensuring employees can easily connect, whether in the office or remotely. The goal is to create environments that promote creativity and teamwork while providing spaces for focused work and personal reflection.

Leadership styles are also undergoing significant changes in this new landscape. As remote work takes precedence, managers are moving away from traditional micromanagement approaches and adopting more supportive, trust-based strategies. This transformation necessitates a shift in mindset for leaders, who must now prioritize outcomes over processes and empower employees to take ownership of their work.

In this context, emotional intelligence and adaptability are essential skills for influential leaders. Managers must cultivate these traits to support their teams effectively while navigating the complexities of remote work. They must be attuned to their team members' challenges and provide the necessary resources and guidance to help them thrive in this environment. For example, a manager who notices a drop in team morale may implement regular check-ins to provide support and encouragement, fostering a sense of connection and commitment among team members.

However, maintaining a strong sense of company culture and camaraderie among remote workers is more critical than ever. Building connections in a virtual environment is challenging, but it is essential for fostering collaboration and teamwork.

Organizations must explore creative ways to engage employees, from virtual team-building activities to informal coffee chats, ensuring that relationships remain strong despite physical distances.

A vibrant and inclusive company culture is vital in retaining top talent and ensuring employees feel valued and connected to their organizations. Companies are discovering innovative methods to create meaningful connections, such as virtual mentoring programs and cross-departmental collaborations. These initiatives strengthen interpersonal bonds and help preserve a sense of identity and belonging within the organization, which can be particularly challenging in a remote setting.

Numerous organizations have successfully adapted to remote work while prioritizing connection and collaboration. Buffer, a social media management platform, is known for its commitment to remote work and transparency. The company regularly publishes its employee engagement surveys, providing insights into how its team members feel and what improvements can be made. Buffer fosters a strong sense of community and engagement among its remote workforce by actively seeking feedback and making adjustments.

Another example is GitLab, an all-remote company emphasizing asynchronous communication and collaboration. By leveraging documentation and transparent processes, GitLab ensures team members can work effectively regardless of time zones. Their comprehensive handbook outlines best practices for communication, collaboration, and work-life balance, serving as a valuable resource for remote employees.

Companies like Zapier, a fully remote organization, have implemented a unique culture of transparency and support. They focus on creating an inclusive work environment by encouraging team members to participate in regular "watercooler" chats, where employees can connect personally. This practice helps foster relationships and allows employees to discuss topics beyond work, further strengthening their connections.

Reflecting on these real-world examples, it becomes evident that successful remote work requires intentionality and commitment from both organizations and employees. By prioritizing adaptability, collaboration, and communication, we can navigate the complexities of remote work and create an environment that supports personal fulfillment and organizational success.

The future of work requires us to rethink our roles, responsibilities, and relationships within our organizations in this rapidly changing landscape. Both employees and employers must embrace the opportunities of remote and hybrid work. By fostering adaptability, communication, and collaboration, we can create work environments that benefit everyone involved.

As we navigate this evolving landscape, let us stay open to change and committed to building workplaces that support personal fulfillment and organizational success. The journey into the new work era is not just about adapting; it is about thriving and harnessing the lessons we learned during this transformative period to create a future where work aligns with our lives, feels connected and valued, and is recognized and celebrated.

Together, we can embrace these changes and opportunities, shaping a more fulfilling and productive professional experience for ourselves and our colleagues. Let us move forward, empowered and ready to redefine what work means, ensuring we survive in this new era and truly thrive.

Navigating the complexities of remote and hybrid work can be daunting. Many individuals struggle with the transition, grappling with feelings of isolation, a blurred work-life balance, and the absence of traditional workplace structures. This book aims to provide practical guidance for success and career growth in the new remote and hybrid workplace, empowering readers to thrive in this new era.

We will explore essential skills and strategies professionals can adopt to excel in remote settings, including effective communication, time management, and self-motivation. Clear and concise communication becomes paramount in an environment where face-to-face interactions are limited. This book will delve into various communication tools and techniques, helping you articulate your thoughts and ideas to foster collaboration and understanding among team members. Furthermore, we will discuss adapting your communication style to accommodate different personalities and preferences, ensuring that all team members feel included and valued.

Additionally, we will cover strategies for managing your time effectively, ensuring that you remain productive while carving out space for breaks and personal time. The importance of setting boundaries cannot be overstated, and we will discuss practical tips for creating a work schedule that allows for flexibility while ensuring that you stay on task. Self-motivation is another critical component of successful remote work. Without the structure of a traditional office, it can be easy to become distracted or lose focus. This book will provide tips on setting personal goals, creating a conducive work environment, and developing routines that enhance productivity.

We will also explore the importance of creating a dedicated workspace that minimizes distractions and maximizes focus. This can involve setting up a specific area in your home that is designated for work and equipping it with the necessary tools and resources to help you stay organized and efficient. Furthermore, we will discuss the significance of regular check-ins with you and your supervisor to assess your progress and recalibrate your goals as necessary. We will discuss the importance of establishing a robust professional network, even when working from a distance. Building and maintaining solid relationships with colleagues and supervisors is essential for career advancement and job satisfaction, and this book will offer practical advice on how to network effectively in a virtual landscape. Networking in a remote environment may differ from traditional settings, but it is still crucial for career growth and development. We will provide insights on leveraging social media platforms, attending virtual conferences, and participating in online communities relevant to your field.

Furthermore, we will discuss the importance of mental health and well-being in remote work. The line between personal and professional life can become blurred, leading to burnout and stress. Recognizing the signs of mental fatigue and understanding how to implement self-care strategies will be pivotal in maintaining a healthy work-life balance. This book will provide insights into mindfulness practices, the importance of taking regular breaks, and techniques for creating boundaries that protect your time.

We will delve into various self-care techniques that can help combat feelings of isolation and anxiety, including mindfulness meditation, exercise routines, and hobbies that promote creativity and relaxation.

As organizations adapt to this new era of work, leaders also play a critical role in shaping the remote work experience. We will explore how managers can foster a culture of inclusivity and support, ensuring all employees feel valued and engaged, regardless of location. This includes setting clear expectations, providing regular feedback, and encouraging open dialogue about challenges and successes in the remote work environment. Effective leadership in this context means being attuned to employees' needs and recognizing their diverse challenges, from isolation to flexibility. Leaders must also model healthy work habits, demonstrating the importance of work-life balance to their teams.

The book will address the implications of technology on remote work. While technology has enabled the shift to remote work, it also poses challenges, such as digital fatigue and the risk of constant connectivity. We will explore how to leverage technology effectively without allowing it to overwhelm employees. Understanding the right tools for collaboration, project management, and communication is essential for maintaining productivity and team cohesion. We will also discuss the potential pitfalls of over-reliance on technology, emphasizing the importance of preserving human connections in a digital world.

As we navigate various technologies that facilitate remote work, we will highlight best practices for virtual meetings, effective use of communication platforms, and tips for managing projects online. It is essential for employees to feel confident and skilled in utilizing these tools to enhance their work experience rather than hinder it.

Finally, we will touch upon the future of work. As remote and hybrid work models become more entrenched, what does this mean for the future of careers and workplaces? We will discuss future trends, such as the gig economy, flexible workspaces, and the increasing emphasis on employee well-being. Preparing for these changes will be crucial for employees and employers wishing to remain competitive and relevant in this evolving landscape. The future of work is not just about location but also about the changing expectations employees have regarding their roles, work environment, and overall career trajectories.
We will analyze emerging trends, such as freelancing and contract work, which have gained popularity due to their flexibility. As companies embrace hybrid models, the traditional full-time role may evolve into a more fluid concept, requiring employees to adapt and continuously develop new skills. This book will encourage readers to be proactive about their career

paths, advocating for lifelong learning and adaptability in an ever-changing job market.

This book is your comprehensive guide to thriving in the new work era. By embracing the changes brought about by remote and hybrid work models, you can unlock new opportunities for personal and professional growth. Whether you are a seasoned remote worker, a newcomer to this way of working, or an employer seeking to foster a productive remote culture, the insights shared within these pages will help you navigate the complexities of this new landscape and set you on the path to success. Welcome to your journey in mastering remote work! Together, we will explore the tools, strategies, and mindsets that will empower you to thrive in this exciting new world of work. As we move forward, remember that adapting to this new era requires flexibility, resilience, and an open mind. The growth opportunities are limitless—let us embrace them together!

This introduction sets the stage for a comprehensive exploration of remote work, guiding you through the necessary skills, strategies, and insights to thrive in this new environment. As we delve deeper into each chapter, you will find actionable advice and real-world examples to help you navigate the challenges and seize the opportunities that remote work presents. Your journey towards mastering the art of remote work begins now!

CHAPTER 1: ADOPTING THE REMOTE MINDSET

Understanding the Remote Work Shift

The work landscape has undergone a seismic shift in recent years, fundamentally altering how we approach our careers and daily responsibilities. With the advent of remote and hybrid work models, professionals are no longer confined to traditional office spaces. Instead, the workplace has expanded beyond the four walls of a physical location, allowing for flexibility and adaptability in ways we could only dream of a decade ago. This transformation has been accelerated by technological advancements, a global pandemic, and a growing demand for work-life balance, prompting organizations to rethink their operational frameworks and strategies.

Remote work is not merely a trend but a permanent fixture in the modern professional world. Employees have discovered the benefits of working from home, such as reduced commuting times, increased autonomy, and the ability to create a personalized work environment. The convenience of managing personal responsibilities alongside professional duties has transformed how individuals view work. With more people prioritizing their well-being, the flexibility to design a workday that accommodates both personal and professional commitments has become highly desirable. This shift has not only empowered employees to tailor their work-life balance. Still, it has also led to a broader acceptance of diverse work arrangements, fostering a more inclusive approach to employment.

The pandemic catalyzed this change, forcing companies worldwide to pivot to remote work almost overnight. According to a report by McKinsey & Company (2021), the pandemic accelerated the adoption of digital technologies by several years, fundamentally changing how businesses operate. This abrupt shift challenged employers and employees to adapt quickly to new technologies and workflows. In the face of adversity, many organizations recognize the resilience and adaptability of their workforce, which has led to long-term changes in how work is conceptualized and executed. For example, organizations that had already embraced some remote work were better positioned to transition entirely, demonstrating the importance of flexibility in modern business strategies.

As companies like Twitter, Facebook, and Shopify announced their commitment to remote work, it became evident that this shift was not just temporary. A survey conducted by Buffer (2021) revealed that 97% of remote workers want to continue working remotely, at least part-time, for the rest of their careers. This overwhelming preference underscores the need for organizations to adapt to a new work culture that prioritizes flexibility and employee well-being. The remote work model is here to stay, reshaping our understanding of work-life balance, productivity, and employee engagement.

The shift toward remote work has also prompted organizations to rethink their physical workspace needs. Many companies are downsizing their office spaces, opting for flexible co-working arrangements or hybrid models that allow employees to choose when to come into the office. For instance, Slack, a company renowned for its collaboration tools, announced its shift to a "digital-first" approach, significantly reducing its office footprint while fostering collaboration among its workforce (Slack Technologies, 2021). This evolution highlights how the traditional boundaries of work dissolve, leading to a more fluid and dynamic approach to how we view our professional lives.

Furthermore, this change in work culture has led to the emergence of new leadership styles. Managers are finding that they must shift from traditional methods of supervision to more supportive and trust-based approaches. This transformation requires managers to focus on results rather than processes, empowering employees to take ownership of their work. In the remote work era, leadership is less about micromanaging and more about providing guidance, resources, and encouragement. As a result, managers must cultivate skills in emotional intelligence and adaptability, ensuring that they can effectively support their teams while navigating the complexities of remote work.

Moreover, as remote work becomes the norm, organizations must adapt to maintain a sense of company culture and camaraderie among employees. Building connections in a virtual environment can be challenging, but it is crucial for fostering collaboration and teamwork. Companies are exploring creative ways to engage employees, from virtual team-building activities to informal coffee chats, ensuring that relationships remain strong despite physical distances. The need for a vibrant and inclusive company culture has never been more pressing, and organizations are discovering innovative methods to create meaningful connections, such as virtual mentoring programs and cross-departmental collaborations. These initiatives strengthen interpersonal bonds and help preserve a sense of identity and belonging within the organization, which can be particularly challenging in a remote setting.

The Importance of Digital Connectivity

Digital connectivity has emerged as a cornerstone of the remote work shift, fundamentally transforming how teams interact and collaborate. With high-speed internet access and advanced communication technologies, employees can work from anywhere worldwide, enabling seamless collaboration and productivity regardless of physical location. Video conferencing platforms such as Zoom and Microsoft Teams have become integral to replacing traditional in-person meetings, providing a digital alternative for face-to-face interactions essential for relationship-building, fostering trust, and maintaining team cohesion. These tools facilitate various interactions, from daily check-ins to brainstorming sessions and project updates, enabling teams to stay connected and aligned on goals and deliverables.

The significance of these platforms in maintaining the fabric of team culture cannot be overstated. Through video calls and instant messaging, team members can share ideas, provide feedback, and work through challenges together, creating a sense of presence even when physically apart. In addition to video conferencing, collaboration tools like Slack, Trello, and Asana have enabled remote teams to manage projects, assign tasks, and track progress, making digital connectivity an essential component of modern work culture. These platforms enhance productivity and ensure transparency and accountability within teams, allowing managers to have clear visibility over project timelines and individual contributions.

However, the heavy reliance on digital tools also introduces a unique set of challenges. As the remote workforce grows, the potential for digital fatigue has become a pressing concern. Many employees are overwhelmed by the sheer volume of virtual meetings and continuous online communication, leading to decreased productivity, increased stress, and diminished morale. Digital fatigue, often called "Zoom fatigue," arises when employees feel mentally and physically exhausted from prolonged screen time and back-to-back video calls. According to a study by Virtira Consulting (2021), approximately 70% of remote workers reported feeling fatigued due to the constant influx of video meetings. This trend highlights the need for organizations to address the strain of digital overload and explore ways to optimize virtual interactions for a healthier work environment.

Organizations must establish best practices for virtual meetings and digital communication to mitigate the adverse effects of digital fatigue. One approach is to set clear agendas for each meeting, ensuring that participants stay focused and that the meeting stays on track. Limiting meeting durations can also help, as shorter, more efficient meetings are often more effective and less draining for attendees. Additionally, encouraging asynchronous communication—where team members collaborate and provide updates without being online simultaneously—can reduce the need for frequent live meetings. This approach minimizes interruptions and allows employees to work at their own pace, fostering a more flexible and balanced work environment. By strategically integrating these practices, organizations can harness the power of digital connectivity while promoting employee well-being, ultimately achieving a more sustainable and productive remote work culture.

A New Era of Work-Life Integration

The traditional concept of work-life balance has transformed significantly in recent years, giving way to the notion of work-life integration. In this new approach, the boundaries between personal and professional life are no longer rigid, allowing for greater fluidity. For many, remote work has enabled a more seamless integration of responsibilities, making it possible to weave personal obligations, such as childcare, health appointments, and household tasks, into the workday without sacrificing productivity. This flexibility allows individuals to meet personal and professional obligations, leading to increased job satisfaction and a more fulfilling lifestyle. However, achieving this integration is complex and requires careful navigation to avoid potential downsides, including burnout, distractions, and productivity challenges.

Work-life integration brings a new set of responsibilities for both employees and organizations. Individuals must establish clear boundaries to prevent professional obligations from consuming personal time while ensuring that personal matters do not intrude excessively on work responsibilities. Without mindful practices, the fluidity of work-life integration can lead to extended work hours, constant connectivity, and, eventually, fatigue. This is why remote workers must set structured routines, prioritize tasks, and designate specific times for work and relaxation to create a healthy balance.

Additionally, personal productivity tools and time-management techniques can be invaluable in helping employees manage their day and reduce the risk of overworking.

Organizations play an equally important role in facilitating successful work-life integration. Companies can support their employees by adopting policies that encourage flexible work hours, giving individuals more control over their schedules. A culture that values employee well-being can make a significant difference in helping workers feel supported in their efforts to balance professional and personal commitments. Providing resources such as mental health days, wellness programs, and access to stress management tools can empower employees to take necessary breaks and recharge. For instance, offering virtual fitness classes, meditation sessions, or access to online counseling services can help employees manage stress effectively.

Furthermore, fostering open conversations about mental health is essential in promoting a supportive work environment. Encouraging employees to discuss mental health openly and without stigma helps to normalize self-care and prevent burnout. Managers can lead by example, taking breaks and respecting after-hours boundaries, demonstrating a healthy work-life integration approach. This also includes encouraging employees to use their vacation days and emphasizing the importance of unplugging from work periodically to maintain productivity and mental well-being. By proactively addressing these aspects, organizations can create an environment where employees feel comfortable balancing their responsibilities, ultimately leading to a happier and more productive workforce. Promoting work-life integration effectively requires a combination of organizational support and personal responsibility. Employees are encouraged to set realistic goals, use technology mindfully, and practice self-care. Meanwhile, organizations can support them by implementing policies that recognize the evolving needs of a modern workforce. As the shift towards remote and hybrid work continues, both parties must work together to refine these practices, ensuring that work-life integration is sustainable and beneficial for all. By embracing this approach, organizations can help employees achieve a fulfilling career while nurturing their well-being, marking a new era in workplace culture.

As we reflect on the changes brought about by the remote work shift, it is clear that the employment landscape will continue to evolve. Organizations that embrace flexibility, prioritize employee well-being, and foster a sense of community will be better positioned to thrive in this new era. The future of work is not just about where we work but how we work together to create inclusive, productive, and fulfilling experiences.
Ultimately, adapting to this new paradigm requires a collective effort from both employers and employees. As we move forward,

let us harness the lessons learned during this transformative period to shape a work environment that empowers individuals, strengthens teams, and promotes overall success in the ever-changing world of work.

Collaboration and Relationship-Building

Collaboration in a remote setting requires intentional effort from both employees and management. Companies can implement collaborative tools like shared documents and project management software to enhance teamwork and ensure everyone can access the necessary information. Platforms like Trello, Asana, and Slack facilitate real-time collaboration, allowing teams to work together efficiently regardless of their physical locations. For instance, a project team can use a shared Google Drive folder to maintain a central repository of files, ensuring all team members can access the most current documents and project updates.

Additionally, organizations should emphasize the importance of relationship-building within remote teams. Managers can encourage team members to take the time to learn about each other's strengths, interests, and working styles. This not only fosters a sense of camaraderie but also enables team members to collaborate more effectively by understanding how to leverage each other's skills. For instance, pairing employees with complementary strengths on projects can lead to more innovative solutions and improved outcomes. By creating a collaborative culture where team members feel comfortable sharing their ideas and feedback, organizations can harness the collective intelligence of their workforce.

Furthermore, mentorship programs can play a significant role in fostering connections among remote workers. By pairing experienced employees with newcomers, organizations can create knowledge-sharing opportunities and personal development. These mentorship relationships can also help build community and support, which is crucial in a remote work environment where individuals may feel isolated. For instance, a company could implement a buddy system that pairs new hires with seasoned employees to help them acclimate to the organization and its culture. This initiative benefits the new employees and empowers mentors to share their expertise and cultivate leadership skills.

Real-World Examples

Numerous organizations have successfully adapted to remote work while prioritizing connection and collaboration. Buffer, a social media management platform, is known for its commitment to remote work and transparency. The company regularly publishes its employee engagement surveys, providing insights into how its team members feel and what improvements can be made. Buffer fosters a strong sense of community and engagement among its remote workforce by actively seeking feedback and adjusting. This approach has been instrumental in maintaining high levels of employee satisfaction, even in a remote setting.

Another example is GitLab, an all-remote company emphasizing asynchronous communication and collaboration. By leveraging documentation and transparent processes, GitLab ensures team members can work effectively regardless of time zones. Their comprehensive handbook outlines best practices for communication, collaboration, and work-life balance, serving as a valuable resource for remote employees. GitLab's commitment to transparency and inclusivity is evident in its organizational practices, as the company actively encourages input from all team members, fostering an environment where everyone feels empowered to contribute.

Additionally, companies like Zapier, a fully remote organization, have implemented a unique culture of transparency and support. They focus on creating an inclusive work environment by encouraging team members to participate in regular "watercooler" chats, where employees can connect personally. This practice helps foster relationships and allows employees to discuss topics beyond work, further strengthening their connections. By offering opportunities for informal interactions, Zapier cultivates a vibrant company culture that transcends the physical limitations of remote work.

Effective digital communication and collaborative practices are essential to successful remote work. By prioritizing regular interactions, fostering relationship-building, and creating an inclusive culture, organizations can overcome the challenges posed by physical distance and empower their teams to thrive in a remote environment. Through real-world examples from leading companies, it is evident that a commitment to connection and collaboration is crucial for building a resilient and engaged remote workforce.

The shift to remote and hybrid work environments presents challenges and opportunities for employees and organizations. This transformation has reshaped the traditional notions of workplace structure and dynamics, leading to new ways of thinking about productivity, collaboration, and employee well-being. As we navigate this evolving landscape, it becomes imperative for professionals to adapt and thrive amid these changes. By understanding the evolution of work culture, developing a resilient mindset, and prioritizing connection and collaboration, individuals can unlock their full potential in this new work environment.

As we delve deeper into this book, we will explore the tools, strategies, and mindsets necessary to navigate the complexities of remote work successfully. Each chapter will provide actionable insights and real-world examples to help you harness the power of remote work, ensuring you are well-equipped to meet the demands of this new era. Whether you are a seasoned remote worker or just starting, the knowledge shared here empowers you to embrace the challenges and seize the opportunities that remote work presents.

Together, we will embrace the changes and opportunities that the new work era brings, paving the way for a more fulfilling and productive professional experience. This journey is not merely about adapting to a new way of working but about thriving in it. It fosters a culture of flexibility, accountability, and innovation within ourselves and our teams. We will explore how to create and sustain an environment where every team member feels valued, connected, and motivated to contribute their best work.

Moreover, as we progress through this book, we will discuss practical strategies for establishing routines that enhance productivity while allowing for personal well-being. We will highlight the importance of utilizing technology effectively, ensuring you remain connected with your colleagues, and streamlining your workflows for maximum efficiency. In today's fast-paced digital world, leveraging technology is no longer a luxury but a necessity for success.

Equally important is maintaining a sense of purpose and connection in a remote work context. Many face the isolation of remote work, making it essential to cultivate relationships and foster a sense of community. Throughout this book, we will discuss how to engage with colleagues meaningfully, establish mentorship relationships, and create networks that provide support and encouragement.

We will also address the importance of work-life balance, mental health, and well-being. These aspects are crucial in ensuring that remote work is sustainable in the long term. Implementing self-care strategies, managing stress effectively, and recognizing the signs of burnout are essential for anyone navigating the remote work landscape. By prioritizing your mental health and establishing healthy boundaries, you can create a work environment that enhances your productivity and promotes your overall well-being.

The journey ahead is one of continuous learning and adaptation. As the landscape of remote work evolves, so must our approaches to managing our careers and teams. It is crucial to remain proactive in seeking new skills, embracing innovation, and staying informed about emerging trends. Doing so will enhance your career prospects and create a thriving organizational culture that can adapt to the future of work.

In conclusion, this book is a comprehensive guide to help you navigate the complexities of remote work. It will equip you with the necessary skills, insights, and tools to thrive in this new era. As we embark on this journey together, let us commit to embracing the possibilities that lie ahead, fostering collaboration, and building a more inclusive and empowering work environment for all. The future of work is bright, and with the right mindset and strategies, we can all be successful in this exciting new landscape.

Sources:

1. Buffer. (2021). *State of Remote Work.*
2. Harvard Business Review. (2020). *How to manage remote direct reports.*
3. Journal of Applied Psychology. (2020). *Self-discipline and performance in remote work settings.*
4. McKinsey & Company. (2021). *COVID-19 has pushed companies over the technology tipping point—and transformed business forever.*
5. McKinsey & Company. (2021). *The Future of Work: What is Next for Remote Work?*
6. Center for Creative Leadership. (2021). *The importance of emotional intelligence in remote leadership.*
7. Slack Technologies. (2021). *Slack's New Approach to Work.*
8. Slack Technologies. (2021). *The future of work is digital.*

CHAPTER 2: DESIGNING YOUR HOME OFFICE FOR PRODUCTIVITY

Setting Up for Success in Your Home Office

Creating an effective home office is not just about finding a corner of your living space to place a desk; it is about cultivating an environment that promotes focus, creativity, and well-being. In the evolving landscape of remote work, understanding the components that contribute to a productive workspace is essential. Consider ergonomics, lighting, noise control, and the right technology tools to set yourself up for success. These elements form the foundation of a workspace that supports your tasks and nurtures your overall health and job satisfaction.

Ergonomics

Ergonomics refers to designing a workspace that fits the user, ultimately enhancing comfort and efficiency while reducing the risk of injury. As many professionals transition to remote work, the importance of ergonomic setups has become increasingly evident. According to the Occupational Safety and Health Administration (OSHA), the ideal ergonomic workstation includes specific recommendations that help prevent discomfort and promote productivity.

Chair Height and Support:

A proper ergonomic chair should provide adequate lumbar support to maintain the spine's natural curve. Adjusting the chair height is crucial so that your feet rest flat on the floor and your knees are at a 90-degree angle. This adjustment helps reduce strain on your lower back and promotes good posture. Furthermore, chairs with adjustable armrests should be considered to prevent shoulder and wrist strain.

Desk Configuration:

Your desk should be at a height that allows your elbows to be at a 90-degree angle while typing. Consider using a sit-stand desk to alternate between sitting and standing throughout the day, which can reduce fatigue and improve energy levels. This flexibility can lead to better circulation and decreased discomfort over long work periods. Additionally, ensure that the desk has enough space for your equipment, including your computer, documents, and other essential tools.

Monitor Positioning:

The top of your computer monitor should be at or slightly below eye level, approximately an arm's length away. This positioning helps minimize neck strain and allows for a comfortable viewing angle. Using monitor risers or adjustable arms can be a practical solution to achieve the right height. It is also beneficial to ensure that your monitor's brightness is adjusted to suit the ambient lighting in your workspace to reduce eye strain.

Implementing these ergonomic principles not only improves comfort but also boosts productivity. For instance, Laura, a project manager, experienced chronic back pain from working in a non-ergonomic setup. After investing in an adjustable chair and a sit-stand desk, she noticed a significant decrease in discomfort, allowing her to concentrate better on her projects. A study published in the *Journal of Occupational Health Psychology* found that employees who utilized ergonomic furniture reported higher job satisfaction and lower levels of discomfort (Sweeney et al., 2018).

Lighting:

Adequate lighting is another critical factor in designing a home office. Poor lighting can lead to eye strain, headaches, and decreased productivity. Ideally, your workspace should take advantage of natural light, which has been shown to boost mood and energy levels. However, if natural light is limited, you can achieve an optimal lighting setup by combining ambient, task, and accent lighting.

Ambient Lighting
This general illumination should fill the room without creating glare. Overhead lights or floor lamps can provide a balanced light source throughout your workspace. Consider using adjustable dimmers to control brightness levels based on your activities and time of day.

Task Lighting
Desk lamps that focus light on specific tasks, such as reading or writing, are essential for preventing eye strain. Ensure your task lighting is adjustable to direct the light exactly where needed. LED desk lamps with adjustable color temperatures can enhance focus and reduce fatigue.

Accent Lighting
While primarily decorative, accent lighting can enhance the overall atmosphere of your workspace, making it more inviting and stimulating creativity. This could include LED strips or spotlights highlighting artwork or motivational quotes in your office. Use warmer tones to create a cozy atmosphere or cooler tones for a more focused, energetic vibe.

According to research from the American Psychological Association (APA, 2020), exposure to natural light has been

linked to improved mood, increased productivity, and even better cognitive performance. Employees who work in well-lit environments report higher satisfaction levels, which translates into enhanced performance. For instance, when Mark transitioned to a home office with ample natural light and appropriate task lighting, his
focus and motivation improved dramatically.

Noise Control:

Managing noise levels is vital for maintaining concentration in a home office, particularly if you share your space with family or roommates. Distractions can arise from everyday household activities, such as conversations, television noise, or outside traffic. Implementing strategies to control noise can significantly enhance your ability to focus and be productive.

Noise-Canceling Headphones
Investing in high-quality noise-canceling headphones can be one of the most effective ways to block distractions. These headphones create a soundproof barrier, allowing you to immerse yourself in your work without interruptions. Look for models with comfortable padding and a long battery life to accommodate extended work sessions.

Soundproofing Your Space
Choose a quiet room for your office. Use rugs, curtains, or sound-absorbing panels to dampen sound. Even simple changes like adding soft furnishings can significantly reduce noise levels. Heavy curtains block outside noise, help regulate temperature, and enhance comfort.

White Noise Machines
These devices generate a consistent background sound that can mask distracting noises. For example, the hum of a fan or the soft sounds of nature can create a calming atmosphere conducive to focus. You can also use apps on your smartphone to produce ambient sounds that help maintain concentration.

Establish Quiet Times:
If you share your living space, communicate with those around you about designated "quiet hours." This agreement can help minimize interruptions and create a more conducive working environment. To reinforce these boundaries, utilize a sign or signal that indicates when you are in a focused work session.

A study published in the *Journal of Environmental Psychology* (2016) found that employees who worked in quieter environments experienced improved focus and reduced stress levels. For example, Lisa, a freelance writer, found that using a white noise machine in her home office allowed her to drown out the sounds of her children playing nearby, significantly increasing her productivity during work hours.

Optimizing Digital Tools

Practical collaboration tools are essential for remote teams in our increasingly digital world. Platforms such as Slack, Zoom, and Asana help streamline communication and project management, ensuring everyone stays connected and informed.

Collaboration Tools:

Slack:

This messaging platform facilitates real-time communication, making it easy for teams to collaborate on projects. With channels for specific topics and direct messaging capabilities, Slack allows for organized discussions and instant sharing of resources. You can integrate various apps into Slack to enhance productivity further, such as Google Drive for document sharing.

Zoom:

As a leading video conferencing tool, Zoom enables virtual meetings and face-to-face interactions, which are vital for maintaining relationships among team members. Features such as breakout rooms and screen sharing enhance the meeting experience, allowing participants to engage more effectively. Make sure to utilize features like recording meetings for later reference and scheduling tools to streamline your calendar.

Asana:

This project management tool helps teams track tasks, deadlines, and project progress. By clearly representing workflows, Asana allows team members to understand their responsibilities and stay accountable. Setting up recurring tasks and deadlines can help maintain momentum on long-term projects.

Integrating these digital tools seamlessly into your work routine enhances productivity. For instance, a marketing team that uses Slack for daily communications, Zoom for weekly check-ins, and Asana for project management can create a cohesive workflow that fosters collaboration and accountability. According to a report by Gartner (2021), organizations that effectively leverage digital collaboration tools are more likely to experience higher employee engagement and improved overall performance.

Managing Distractions

In a remote work environment, distractions can be plentiful, so implementing strategies that minimize interruptions and maximize focus is crucial. Here are some proven techniques to help you stay on track:

1. Establish Clear Boundaries:
   Communicate your work hours to family members and friends, ensuring they understand when you are unavailable. Setting boundaries can help create a more focused work environment and reduce interruptions. Consider posting your schedule in a visible area to remind others of your dedicated work hours.

2. Create a Dedicated Workspace:
   Designate a specific area in your home for work. This separation can help signal to your brain that it is time to focus, making switching to work mode easier. Ensure your workspace is free from distractions like TV or non-work-related items.
3. Use the Pomodoro Technique:
   This time management method involves working for a set period (typically 25 minutes) followed by a short break (5 minutes). This approach can help maintain focus and prevent burnout. Many find that breaking their work into manageable chunks increases concentration and productivity. Consider using apps that track your Pomodoro sessions to help keep you accountable.
4. Limit Social Media Use:
   Social media can be a significant distraction. Use website blockers during work hours to minimize temptations and focus on your tasks. Setting specific times for social media checks can help you remain connected without allowing it to interfere with your productivity.
5. Mindfulness Practices:
   Incorporating mindfulness techniques, such as deep breathing or meditation, into your daily routine can help reduce stress and improve focus. Taking a few minutes to center yourself before diving into work can significantly affect productivity. You might find guided meditation apps helpful for establishing a consistent practice.

Implementing these strategies in real life can lead to significant improvements in productivity and job satisfaction. For example, after

 integrating ergonomic furniture, optimal lighting, and effective noise control, many employees have reported enhanced focus and reduced discomfort. Companies encouraging team-building activities and utilizing digital collaboration tools have also seen increased engagement and productivity among their remote workforce. By setting up a thoughtful and practical home office, you position yourself for success in the evolving world of remote work.

Creating a productive home office is more than just a practical necessity; it is a strategic investment in your personal and professional success. By paying attention to ergonomics, lighting, noise control, and the digital tools you utilize, you can craft a workspace that enhances your productivity and supports your overall well-being. Remember that the goal is to create an environment that fosters focus, creativity, and engagement, allowing you to navigate the challenges of remote work with confidence and effectiveness. Implementing these strategies will lead to a more satisfying and successful remote work experience, setting you on a path to achieving your professional goals.

Numerous organizations have successfully adapted their home office designs to promote productivity. For example, the software company Trello emphasizes the importance of workspace design and offers tips for creating a productive home office. They encourage employees to personalize their workspaces, ensuring they feel comfortable and motivated in their environments (Trello, 2021). Similarly, GitHub has adopted a flexible approach to remote work, allowing employees to design their workspaces to suit their needs. The company emphasizes the importance of finding an environment that fosters productivity, whether creating a quiet space for deep work or an open area for collaboration with team members (GitHub, 2021).

Additionally, companies like Zapier, a fully remote organization, have implemented a unique culture of transparency and support. They focus on creating an inclusive work environment by encouraging team members to participate in regular "watercooler" chats, where employees can connect personally. This practice helps foster relationships and allows employees to discuss topics beyond work, further strengthening their connections.

References

1. Occupational Safety and Health Administration (OSHA). (n.d.). *Computer Workstations: Ergonomics.* Retrieved from https://www.osha.gov/ergonomics
2. American Psychological Association. (2018). *The impact of light on well-being.* Retrieved from https://www.apa.org
3. Harvard Business Review. (2020). *How to manage remote direct reports.* Retrieved from https://hbr.org/2020/03/how-to-manage-remote-direct-reports
4. Center for Creative Leadership. (2021). *The importance of emotional intelligence in remote leadership.* Retrieved from https://www.ccl.org/articles/leading-effectively-articles/emotional-intelligence-in-remote-leadership/
5. Journal of Applied Psychology. (2020). *Self-discipline and performance in remote work settings.* Retrieved from https://www.apa.org/pubs/journals/apl
6. Buffer. (2021). *State of Remote Work 2021.* Retrieved from https://buffer.com/state-of-remote-work
7. GitHub. (2021). *Remote work.* Retrieved from https://github.com/about
8. Trello. (2021). *How to create a productive home office.* Retrieved from https://trello.com

CHAPTER 3: MAXIMIZING PRODUCTIVITY IN A HYBRID WORLD

The rise of hybrid work models presents unique challenges and opportunities for employees and organizations. This chapter explores key strategies for maximizing productivity in a hybrid environment, focusing on mastering time management, balancing hybrid schedules, and ensuring visibility and value in your role.

Mastering Time Management

Effective time management is essential for thriving in a hybrid work model, where the blend of remote and in-office work can create challenges in maintaining focus and productivity. Individuals can harness their time more efficiently by employing specific techniques and aligning their work with personal and professional goals.

The Pomodoro Technique

The Pomodoro Technique is a time management method developed by Francesco Cirillo in the late 1980s. Named after the Italian word for "tomato" (inspired by the tomato-shaped kitchen timer Cirillo used), this technique breaks down work into focused intervals called "Pomodoros," each followed by a short break. The method aims to enhance concentration, maintain energy levels, and reduce mental fatigue, making it especially beneficial for lengthy projects or tasks requiring sustained focus.

How It Works

Choose a Task:
Begin by selecting a specific task or small set of tasks to accomplish. These could include writing an article, working through a report, coding, studying, or organizing files.
Try to make the task manageable within the length of a single Pomodoro (50 minutes in this extended version). If the task seems too large, break it into smaller, achievable parts to fit into each session.

Set a Timer for 50 Minutes:
Setting a timer is a core part of the Pomodoro Technique. In this version, set the timer for 50 minutes, giving yourself a longer focused work session.
Commit to work uninterruptedly on your task for the entire 50 minutes. Knowing there is a countdown can provide a sense of urgency and encourage a deeper level of focus.

Work Until the Timer Rings:
During these 50 minutes, focus solely on the task at hand. Avoid distractions like checking emails, answering phone calls, or browsing social media.
If a distraction arises, quickly jot it down on a "Distraction List" to address later. This list helps you avoid losing focus while allowing you to revisit these thoughts after the Pomodoro session.

Take a 20-Minute Break:
Once the timer rings, take a 20-minute break. Use this time to recharge both mentally and physically.
Consider using the break for stretching, grabbing a snack,

walking around, or engaging in a mindfulness exercise. The key is to step away from your workspace to give your brain a real rest, which helps prevent burnout.

Repeat:
After four Pomodoros (approximately 200 minutes of work time), take a more extended break of 60 to 120 minutes.
This extended break is essential for recovering your mental and physical energy. Use this time to engage in more restful or enjoyable activities, like walking outside, meditating, reading, or having a meal.

Why the Pomodoro Technique Works

The Pomodoro Technique is based on focus, rhythm, and regular rest principles. Working in shorter intervals reduces the likelihood of experiencing cognitive fatigue, which can lead to procrastination, errors, and stress. Here is how this technique addresses common productivity issues:

Combats Mental Fatigue: The longer Pomodoro interval (50 minutes) allows for deep work, while regular breaks prevent burnout. When you take structured breaks, you come back refreshed and ready to tackle the next session with renewed energy.

Encourages Focused Work: The dedicated timer discourages multitasking and creates a sense of urgency to complete a task within the set time frame, helping eliminate unnecessary distractions.

Improves Task Management: Breaking down tasks into Pomodoros helps you estimate how long different tasks take, allowing you to improve time management and plan your workload more effectively over time.

Tips for Implementing the Pomodoro Technique

Find the Right Environment:

Choose a workspace free of distractions. Consider using noise-canceling headphones or background music to help you concentrate.

Customize Your Pomodoro Length:
Some people find that more than 50 minutes is needed to be shorter, depending on the nature of their tasks. Experiment with shorter or longer intervals to find what works best for you.

Use Technology to Support the Process:
Consider using Pomodoro-specific apps or digital timers that automatically alternate between work and break periods. Many apps also track your Pomodoros over time, allowing you to analyze your productivity patterns.

Track Your Sessions:
At the end of each Pomodoro, mark it down in a log. This tracking will give you insight into your productivity and help you identify any patterns in your work habits.

Reflect and Adjust:
After a few days or weeks of using the Pomodoro Technique, reflect on its effectiveness for your workflow. If needed, adjust the length of your work sessions, break times, or tasks.

Jenna, a marketing specialist working remotely, discovered the Pomodoro Technique during a particularly demanding project. At first, she struggled to stay focused with her children at home, and frequent notifications interrupted her concentration. After trying the Pomodoro Technique, Jenna found that she was more disciplined and productive. By setting 50-minute Pomodoro sessions, she could complete tasks faster without sacrificing quality, and she used her breaks to reconnect with her family, get fresh air, and reset for the next round of work.

Benefits of the Pomodoro Technique

- **Enhanced Concentration**: Knowing you only must focus for a set time helps your mind stay on task

without becoming overwhelmed.
- **Reduced Stress and Burnout**: Regular, structured breaks prevent mental and physical fatigue, promoting a sustainable work pace.
- **Improved Quality of Work**: By working with undivided attention, many users make fewer mistakes and produce higher-quality work.
- **Greater Awareness of Time**: The technique helps you become more aware of how you spend your time and what tasks require the most focus, allowing for better planning.

Time-Blocking for Hybrid Work Success

Time-blocking is a highly effective strategy for managing time in a hybrid work environment. This technique involves scheduling specific blocks of time on your calendar for dedicated work, meetings, and personal breaks. Treating these time slots as unmissable appointments can enhance accountability, minimize the chances of multitasking, and improve overall productivity. Time-blocking helps manage work-related tasks and fosters better work-life balance by creating clear boundaries between professional and personal commitments.

Time-blocking is based on assigning specific time intervals for distinct activities rather than working reactively throughout the day. This structured approach allows you to focus intensely on one task at a time, reducing the mental strain caused by constant task-switching. It is instrumental in hybrid work settings, where balancing in-office responsibilities with remote tasks can be challenging.

How to Implement Time-Blocking

Assess Your Tasks:

Start by listing all the tasks you must complete for the week, including work-related and personal commitments. Be comprehensive in your list, considering meetings, deadlines, project work, emails, administrative tasks, and individual activities like exercise or errands.

Group tasks into categories, such as "high priority," "routine," and "personal." This categorization will help you understand which tasks require more focus and which can be completed during lower-energy periods.

Include recurring daily or weekly tasks, such as checking emails or attending team meetings. A clear overview of all commitments will make the time-blocking process more effective.

Allocate Time for Each Task:
Estimate how long each task will take and allocate specific blocks of time on your calendar for them. Be realistic about your estimates; it is better to overestimate the time needed than to undercut yourself, which can lead to rushed work and stress.

Divide your day into different blocks of time, such as 30-minute, 60-minute, or 90-minute intervals, depending on the nature of the tasks. For example, you might schedule 90 minutes for focused writing or analysis, while meetings might be allotted 30 to 60 minutes.

Include buffer times between tasks, allowing unexpected delays or quick breaks to reset. These buffers can prevent schedule overruns and reduce the pressure of moving immediately from one task to another.

Prioritize High-Impact Tasks:
Identify your high-priority tasks and schedule them during peak productivity hours, typically when you have the most energy and focus. This ensures that your most crucial work receives the best mental resources.

For example, if you are most productive in the morning, allocate blocks for strategic planning, creative work, or complex problem-solving. Leave less demanding tasks, like checking emails or administrative work, for later in the day when your energy levels might be lower.

Use the Eisenhower Matrix (urgent vs. essential) to determine which tasks should be prioritized. Focus on urgent and important tasks first, then move to important but non-urgent ones.

Minimize Distractions During Time Blocks:
During each time block, focus solely on the assigned task. Minimize distractions by silencing notifications, closing unnecessary browser tabs, and setting your status to "do not disturb" on communication platforms like Slack or Teams.

Consider using digital tools like Focus@Will, which plays concentration-enhancing music, or website blockers like StayFocusd to prevent access to distracting websites during work intervals.

If working from a home office, communicate your time-blocking schedule to household members, letting them know when you should not be disturbed. For in-office days, use noise-canceling headphones to create a more focused environment.

Include Personal Time and Breaks:
Time-blocking is not just for work-related tasks—it is also a great way to ensure you dedicate time to personal activities, such as exercise, hobbies, or relaxation. Include blocks for lunch, a short walk, or even a coffee break to recharge between work sessions.

Incorporating personal time into your schedule helps maintain a balanced work-life dynamic and prevents burnout. For example, schedule a 30-minute walk after lunch or a 20-minute meditation break in the mid-afternoon.

Use the Pomodoro Technique for micro time-blocking: work for 25 minutes, then take a 5-minute break. This technique can help maintain focus and energy levels throughout the day.

Evaluate and Adjust Time Blocks Regularly:

Review your time-blocking schedule at the end of each week to see what worked well and what did not. Did specific tasks require more time than anticipated? Were some blocks frequently interrupted? Use these insights to refine your time-blocking approach for the following week.

Adjust time blocks based on changing priorities or deadlines. Flexibility is critical to effective time-blocking, as rigid adherence to a schedule can become counterproductive if it does not accommodate new developments or urgent tasks.

Tips for Maximizing the Benefits of Time-Blocking

1. **Start with a Daily Planning Session**:

Begin each day with a 10—to 15-minute planning session. Review your time-blocking schedule and adjust to urgent tasks or unexpected changes. This morning routine sets a clear direction for the day, helping you transition smoothly into work mode.

2. **Batch Similar Tasks Together**:

Batch similar tasks into one-time blocks to maintain momentum and reduce mental switching costs. For example, group emails, quick calls, and other communication tasks can be put into one block, allowing you to focus on more profound work during different intervals.

Batching also applies to meetings—try to schedule them back-to-back in one block rather than spreading them throughout the day, which can fragment focus and reduce productivity.

3. **Use Color Coding for Clarity**:

Use color coding in your digital calendar to differentiate between types of tasks, such as work tasks, personal activities, meetings, or breaks. This visual organization makes it easier to identify priorities and balance your schedule at a glance.

For example, green is used for high-priority work tasks, blue for meetings, yellow for personal time, and red for urgent tasks. This helps with organization and motivates by clearly displaying dedicated personal and break times.

   4. **Integrate Time-Blocking with Other Productivity Techniques**:

Combine time-blocking with other productivity strategies like the Getting Things Done (GTD) method, which emphasizes capturing, clarifying, organizing, reflecting, and engaging with tasks. Use time blocks to implement GTD steps, such as allocating blocks for processing emails or brainstorming new ideas.

Use time-blocking in conjunction with weekly and monthly planning. Dedicate specific blocks for reviewing goals, evaluating progress, and setting new priorities to ensure alignment with broader objectives.

   5. **Stay Flexible and Adaptable**:

While time-blocking promotes structure, it is essential to remain flexible. Adjust your blocks accordingly if an urgent issue or task takes longer. The key to successful time-blocking is not rigidity but strategic adaptability—the ability to shift blocks while maintaining a sense of direction.

Benefits of Time-Blocking

Time-blocking not only aids in managing your workload but also contributes to a better work-life balance. As you create boundaries around your time, you can carve out space for personal activities without feeling overwhelmed by work obligations. Some of the key benefits include:

   1. **Increased Focus and Efficiency**:

By dedicating specific time to each task, time-blocking enhances focus, reduces distractions, and minimizes the mental fatigue associated with multitasking.

Knowing precisely what you will be working on at any given time increases momentum and helps prevent procrastination, as there is less room for indecision about which task to tackle next.

2. **Reduced Stress and Overwhelm**:

The structured approach of time-blocking helps break down large projects into smaller, manageable steps, reducing feelings of overwhelm and creating a sense of progress.

Including personal time and breaks in your schedule can maintain mental and physical well-being, prevent burnout, and promote a healthier balance between work and personal life.

3. **Greater Accountability**:

Treating each time block as an appointment enhances accountability. Knowing that you have allocated specific time for a task increases the likelihood of completing it within that window, leading to more consistent performance and task completion.

When shared with a team, time-blocking can improve collaboration and transparency, as colleagues can see your availability and respect your focused work times.

4. **Improved Work-Life Integration**:

Time-blocking creates clear boundaries between work and personal time, ensuring that professional commitments do not infringe on individual activities. This balanced approach enhances well-being and supports a sustainable work rhythm in hybrid environments.

Time-blocking is a versatile and effective strategy for enhancing productivity, focus, and work-life balance in hybrid work environments. By clearly allocating time for tasks, meetings, and personal activities, remote and hybrid workers can manage their schedules more effectively and maintain a healthier, more balanced approach to work and personal life. By incorporating time-blocking into your routine, you can boost productivity while ensuring you have time for the things that matter most.

Prioritization Strategies for Hybrid Work Success

Managing multiple responsibilities in a hybrid work setting can quickly become overwhelming, especially when juggling in-office tasks, remote projects, meetings, and personal commitments. Adopting effective prioritization strategies is essential for focusing on what truly matters, enhancing productivity, and achieving long-term goals. By strategically determining which tasks to tackle first, you can optimize your workflow, reduce stress, and achieve a better work-life balance.

Understanding the Eisenhower Matrix

The Eisenhower Matrix is one of the most effective tools for prioritization. It categorizes tasks into four distinct quadrants based on their urgency and importance, enabling you to focus on the tasks with the highest impact on your goals. Here is a detailed look at each quadrant and how to apply it:

1. Urgent and Important:

Tasks in this quadrant require immediate attention and have significant consequences if not addressed promptly. These are often crisis-driven tasks, such as meeting tight deadlines, handling client emergencies, or addressing critical issues that impact business operations.

Examples include responding to urgent customer complaints, finalizing a project for an imminent deadline, or solving unexpected technical problems that disrupt workflows.

Action Plan: Prioritize these tasks and aim to complete them immediately. Allocate focused time blocks without distractions to ensure that they are handled efficiently. Consider using tools like the Pomodoro Technique to focus intensely on high-priority tasks while avoiding burnout.

Preventive Measures: While some tasks in this quadrant are unavoidable, others result from poor planning. To reduce the frequency of urgent and essential tasks, consider proactive strategies like regular project check-ins, early deadline setting, and clear communication with team members.

2. Necessary but Not Urgent:

Tasks in this quadrant contribute significantly to long-term goals but do not require immediate action. These tasks are crucial for growth and improvement, including strategic planning, skill development, building relationships, and self-care routines.

Examples include setting up a new project framework, attending professional development courses, strategic brainstorming, or establishing long-term client relationships.

Action Plan: Schedule these tasks into your calendar and treat them as non-negotiable appointments. Although they do not have immediate deadlines, they are fundamental for personal and professional growth. By consistently allocating time to these tasks, you ensure steady progress toward long-term goals. Techniques for Success: Use tools like SMART goals (Specific, Measurable, Achievable, Relevant, and Time-bound) to break down these tasks into actionable steps. Regularly review your progress and adjust your plans as needed. For example, if you are learning a new skill, set weekly goals for study hours or completed lessons to maintain momentum.

3. Urgent but Not Important:

These tasks require attention but only contribute indirectly to your long-term goals. They often result from other people's priorities or administrative duties, such as non-essential meetings, last-minute requests, or urgent but routine emails.

Examples include handling administrative paperwork, addressing minor technical issues, or responding to non-critical emails that do not contribute to core objectives.

Action Plan: Delegate these tasks whenever possible. If delegation is not an option, try to handle them quickly without allowing them to disrupt your workflow. For instance, similar tasks can be grouped and allocated a specific time block to hold them simultaneously, minimizing their impact on productivity. Minimizing Disruptions: Use automated tools to manage these tasks more effectively. For instance, use email filters to sort non-essential messages, set up auto-responses for standard requests, or use scheduling tools to manage meetings more efficiently. The key is ensuring these tasks consume less time or energy than necessary.

4. Neither Urgent nor Important:

Tasks in this quadrant neither contribute to your goals nor require immediate attention. These are often distractions or activities that provide little to no value to your work or personal growth.

Examples include unnecessary meetings, excessive scrolling on social media, lengthy discussions with no clear agenda, or handling tasks that could be automated.

Action Plan: Consider eliminating these tasks from your to-do list altogether. If elimination is impossible, try to limit the time spent on them to the bare minimum. For example, schedule a "distraction block" where you allow yourself to engage with these activities for a set time, ensuring they do not interfere with more important work.

Fostering Focus: Create a "stop-doing list" alongside your to-do list. This list should identify tasks, behaviors, or commitments that no longer serve your goals. Periodically review your stop-doing list to ensure that you are actively eliminating low-value activities from your routine.

Advanced Prioritization Techniques

In addition to the Eisenhower Matrix, several other techniques can further enhance your prioritization efforts, especially in a hybrid work environment:

ABC Method:

The ABC method categorizes tasks based on their impact:
Tasks are the most critical and must be completed first.
B tasks are essential but can be tackled after A functions.
C tasks are less critical and can be addressed later.
This method helps create a clear order of priority, especially when dealing with an extensive list of tasks. It is beneficial when combined with time-blocking, allowing you to allocate dedicated time for each category throughout the day.

Eat the Frog Technique:

This technique emphasizes completing the most challenging or important task (the "frog") first thing in the morning. By tackling the most daunting task early, you build momentum for the rest of the day and reduce procrastination.

Identify your "frog" by reviewing the tasks in your urgent and essential quadrant and choose the one with the highest impact. Completing this task sets a positive tone for the day and often makes the remaining tasks feel more manageable.

Pareto Principle (80/20 Rule):

The Pareto Principle suggests that 80% of your results come from 20% of your efforts. When applied to prioritization, it encourages focusing on the few tasks that yield the most significant outcomes.

Identify the tasks that have the greatest impact on your work. For example, if you are working on a project, focus on the key activities that contribute most to project completion, such as strategic planning or stakeholder communication. By prioritizing these tasks, you ensure that your efforts are directed toward achieving meaningful results.

Kanban System:

The Kanban system is a visual workflow management tool that helps track tasks from start to finish. It involves creating columns labeled "To Do," "In Progress," and "Done," making it easier to manage priorities and see the status of each task.

Use digital tools like Trello or physical boards to create a Kanban system that tracks tasks based on priority and progress. This approach provides a clear visual representation of your workload, helping you stay organized and focused on high-priority tasks.

Daily and Weekly Reviews:
Conducting daily and weekly reviews is an essential part of effective prioritization. At the end of each day, review what you've accomplished and adjust your priorities for the next day. This routine helps ensure that you are continuously aligned with your goals.

During weekly reviews, assess your progress toward long-term objectives and adjust your task list accordingly. Weekly reviews also offer an opportunity to identify any urgent tasks that have emerged and need to be addressed in the upcoming week.

Implementing Prioritization Strategies in Hybrid Work

1. **Leverage Digital Tools for Prioritization**:

Tools like Asana, Monday.com, and Microsoft To-Do allow for digital prioritization, offering task labeling, due dates, and progress tracking features. These tools can integrate with calendars and communication platforms, making it easier to manage priorities across remote and in-office settings.

Use calendar features to mark time slots for urgent and essential tasks, ensuring you allocate sufficient time for high-priority work without interruptions.

2. **Communicate Priorities Clearly**:

Clear communication is vital for effective prioritization in a hybrid environment. Update your team regularly on your current priorities, especially when working remotely. Use team meetings or project management tools to ensure alignment on task importance and deadlines.

When collaborating with colleagues, be transparent about

which tasks are in your "urgent and important" quadrant and seek their input to avoid misalignment. This collaborative approach ensures that the team understands shared priorities and can effectively coordinate efforts.

3. **Adapt to Changing Priorities**:

In a hybrid work environment, priorities can shift rapidly due to changing circumstances, urgent requests, or new deadlines. Be prepared to adjust your prioritization strategies accordingly. Reassess tasks regularly to focus on what matters most, even as new demands arise.

Practice flexibility by maintaining a "priority buffer" in your schedule. This buffer allows unexpected tasks to occur without disrupting your planned priorities.

Benefits of Effective Prioritization

Adopting effective prioritization strategies offers several benefits that enhance both professional performance and personal well-being:

Increased Productivity:

Focusing on high-priority tasks ensures you are directing your energy toward the most impactful activities, leading to greater productivity and efficiency. Completing essential tasks first often creates a sense of accomplishment, motivating you to tackle the rest of your workload with confidence.

Reduced Stress and Overwhelm:

A clear prioritization strategy allows you to manage your workload more effectively and prevent being overwhelmed by competing demands. Knowing exactly where to focus helps reduce decision fatigue and creates a sense of control over your schedule.

Better Work-Life Balance:

Prioritization allows for intentional time management, enabling you to allocate sufficient time for personal activities and self-care. By aligning your work tasks with long-term goals, you create space for meaningful personal pursuits, contributing to a healthier work-life balance.

Improved Goal Achievement:
Prioritizing tasks that align with your long-term goals ensures steady progress toward those objectives. Consistently focusing on what matters accelerates goal achievement and fosters a sense of purpose in remote and in-office work settings.

Effective prioritization is essential for navigating the complexities of hybrid work. Using strategies like the Eisenhower Matrix, ABC method, and daily reviews, you can manage your workload efficiently, focus on meaningful tasks, and better balance professional and personal commitments. Consistent practice makes prioritization second nature, leading to enhanced productivity, reduced stress, and long-term success.

Balancing Hybrid Schedules

Navigating a hybrid work schedule requires careful planning and flexibility. Many employees are now balancing remote workdays with in-office responsibilities, making it essential to create a strategy that maximizes productivity while maintaining work-life balance.

Planning Ahead

Effective planning is critical to thriving in a hybrid environment. At the beginning of each week, take some time to review your commitments and create a clear plan for how you will allocate your time. Consider the following tips:

Establish a Routine: Develop a consistent daily routine with specific work hours, break times, and personal activities. A well-defined schedule can help you transition smoothly between remote and in-office work.

Coordinate with Your Team: Communicate with your colleagues about in-office days and meeting schedules. Understanding when your team will be present can help you maximize collaboration and engagement during those times.

Use a Shared Calendar: Utilize a shared calendar tool to inform everyone of your availability and commitments. This transparency fosters better communication and collaboration among team members.

By planning, you can ensure that you stay organized and focused, ultimately enhancing your productivity and job satisfaction.

Flexibility and Adaptability

While planning is essential, so is the ability to adapt to changing circumstances. Hybrid work environments can present unexpected challenges, from last-minute meetings to changes in project priorities. Embracing flexibility allows you to respond to these challenges without feeling overwhelmed.

Practice Mindfulness: Incorporating mindfulness techniques into your daily routine can help you remain present and focused, even amidst change. Taking a few moments to breathe deeply or meditate can clear your mind and prepare you for the task.

Stay Open to Change: Accept that plans may need to shift based on team dynamics or external factors. By remaining open to change, you can adjust your schedule without added stress, allowing you to maintain productivity.

For example, a project manager named Michael learned to embrace flexibility in his hybrid work routine. When a last-minute client meeting required him to adjust his work schedule, he quickly shifted his priorities without feeling overwhelmed. This adaptability allowed him to remain productive and maintain positive relationships with his clients and team.

Staying Visible and Valued

In a hybrid work model, staying visible and demonstrating your value to the organization is essential for career advancement. With employees working remotely and in the office, it can be challenging to maintain a sense of connection and recognition.

Building Relationships in a Hybrid Environment

Building relationships with colleagues and supervisors is vital in a hybrid work environment. Strong interpersonal connections enhance collaboration, boost morale, and create a supportive network that can help you navigate the challenges of remote work. Here are several strategies to cultivate these meaningful relationships:

Regular Check-Ins:

Schedule regular check-ins with your manager to discuss your progress, challenges, and goals. These conversations inform your supervisor and allow you to showcase your achievements and contributions. Consistent communication fosters trust and transparency, essential in a hybrid setting with limited face-to-face interactions. Utilize these check-ins to seek project guidance and clarify expectations, ensuring alignment with your manager's vision. Additionally, this allows one to express concerns or seek feedback, promoting a culture of openness and support.

For example, consider implementing a bi-weekly check-in schedule where you and your manager can set aside dedicated time to discuss critical projects, upcoming deadlines, and personal development goals. This demonstrates your initiative, helps your manager stay engaged with your work, and better understand your aspirations. By actively participating in these discussions, you reinforce your commitment to your role and foster a more robust professional relationship.

Engage in Team Activities:

Participate in team-building activities and virtual events to strengthen relationships with colleagues. These interactions foster camaraderie and create a supportive network, enhancing your overall work experience. Engaging in social activities, even in a virtual format, allows team members to connect personally, breaking down barriers that remote work can create.

Look for opportunities to join team challenges, virtual coffee breaks, or social hours where you can interact with colleagues outside of work-related discussions. For instance, you could suggest a themed trivia night or a book club, encouraging team members to share their interests and experiences. These activities promote a sense of belonging and encourage collaboration and creativity, making the work environment more enjoyable and productive.

Additionally, consider creating a shared online space where team members can share personal updates, hobbies, or achievements. This could be a dedicated channel on your team's collaboration platform where everyone is encouraged to post about non-work-related interests. Sharing personal stories and experiences builds a stronger community and fosters deeper connections among team members.

Be Proactive:

Take the initiative to reach out to colleagues for collaboration or to share ideas. Being proactive demonstrates your engagement and willingness to contribute to the team's success. Whether proposing a joint project, helping with a challenging task, or sharing insights from a recent training, taking the initiative shows that you are invested in the team's objectives.

For example, if you notice a colleague struggling with a project, reach out to offer support or share resources that might help. Alternatively, if you have an idea for improving a team process, do not hesitate to voice your thoughts during meetings or one-on-one conversations. This proactive approach helps your colleagues and positions you as a valuable team player committed to the group's success.

Furthermore, consider scheduling informal "lunch and learn" sessions where team members can share their expertise or insights on specific topics. This will facilitate knowledge sharing and encourage interaction and collaboration, creating a more cohesive team environment.

Utilize Virtual Tools:

Make the most of virtual communication tools to enhance your interactions with colleagues. Platforms like Slack, Microsoft Teams, and Zoom offer various features that can help maintain connections. Use video calls for essential discussions to convey tone and body language more effectively, as these cues can often be lost in written communication. Video meetings also foster a more personal connection compared to text-based exchanges.

Additionally, consider using collaborative tools such as shared documents or project management software to collaborate in real-time. This environment can enhance teamwork and ensure everyone is on the same page, allowing for seamless contributions from all team members, regardless of their physical location.

Show Appreciation:

Remember to underestimate the power of gratitude in building relationships. Regularly expressing appreciation for your colleagues' efforts can go a long way in fostering a positive work environment. A simple "thank you" or a shout-out during a team meeting can make individuals feel valued and recognized for their contributions.

Consider creating a recognition program within your team. Colleagues can nominate each other for monthly or quarterly awards based on their contributions. This encourages a culture of appreciation and strengthens bonds among team members by celebrating each other's successes.

Showcasing Your Work in a Hybrid Environment

Demonstrating your value in a hybrid work environment requires intentional effort and strategic communication. In this evolving landscape, where physical presence is often limited, the ability to effectively showcase your contributions can significantly enhance your professional reputation and career advancement. Here are some tactics to consider implementing:

Document Your Achievements:

Keeping a comprehensive record of your accomplishments is crucial. This can include project completions, successful presentations, innovative ideas, and any metrics that showcase your performance. Regularly share these achievements with your manager or team to highlight your contributions. Consider creating a digital portfolio or a simple document outlining your key projects and results, including any recognition from peers or clients. This is a personal motivator and provides a concrete way to articulate your value during performance reviews or one-on-one meetings.

Leverage Technology:

Technology is pivotal in facilitating communication and collaboration in a hybrid work model. Use collaboration tools like Slack, Microsoft Teams, or Asana to share updates, progress reports, and results with your team. These platforms enable you to keep everyone informed about your work, fostering transparency and reinforcing your value to the organization. Consider setting up regular check-ins or updates in shared channels, allowing your team to celebrate successes and brainstorm solutions collectively. You can maintain visibility and remind your colleagues of your contributions by showcasing your work through these channels, even when you are not in the same physical space.

Seek Feedback:

Actively seeking feedback is essential for continuous improvement and growth. Engage with colleagues and supervisors to identify areas to enhance your performance or develop new skills. Regularly asking for feedback demonstrates your commitment to personal and professional development, showcasing your willingness to learn and adapt. Create an open line of communication where team members can provide constructive feedback in a respectful and supportive manner. For instance, after completing a project, consider conducting a brief retrospective session to discuss what went well and what could be improved. This helps you gain insights into your work and encourages a culture of collaboration and growth within your team.

Share Success Stories:

Beyond documenting achievements, sharing specific success stories can illustrate your impact within the organization. Whether through a team meeting, a newsletter, or internal communications, take the initiative to narrate how your efforts contributed to achieving team or company goals. For example, if you implemented a new process that improved efficiency, detail the challenges faced, the solutions you proposed, and the measurable outcomes achieved. This storytelling approach highlights your contributions and inspires your colleagues to recognize the value of their work and promote a positive work culture.

Engage in Collaborative Projects:

Look for opportunities to participate in cross-functional teams or collaborative projects. Engaging with different departments allows you to showcase your skills and build relationships beyond your immediate team. You can demonstrate your versatility and ability to work well with others by actively contributing to diverse initiatives. For instance, if you are a marketing professional, collaborating with the sales or product development teams can provide a broader perspective on the company's objectives and challenges, showcasing your holistic understanding of the business.

Utilize Performance Metrics:

In addition to qualitative achievements, leverage quantitative metrics to support your contributions. Many organizations use key performance indicators (KPIs) to measure success. You can present a data-driven case for your contributions by aligning your work with these metrics. For example, if your role is in sales, track your numbers against targets and showcase how your efforts helped exceed expectations. Being able to present complex data not only validates your work but also enhances your credibility in discussions with management.

Foster Team Spirit:

Encourage and support your colleagues in showcasing their work as well. By creating a culture of recognition within your team, you can collectively highlight everyone's contributions, making it easier for individuals to gain visibility. Consider implementing a "shout-out" system where team members can publicly recognize each other's efforts during meetings or through internal channels. This strengthens team bonds and emphasizes a collaborative spirit where everyone's contributions are valued.

Real-World Example

For instance, Sarah, a remote sales representative, regularly shared her monthly sales reports with her manager and team. By proactively showcasing her results and contributions, she highlighted her value and fostered a sense of accountability and teamwork within her group. Moreover, Sarah initiated a monthly team meeting to discuss collective goals and share best practices, further promoting collaboration and shared success.

Maximizing productivity in a hybrid world requires effective time management, a balanced approach to work schedules, and intentional efforts to stay visible and valued. Employees can enhance their focus and efficiency by mastering techniques like the Pomodoro Technique and time-blocking. Building relationships and showcasing achievements are crucial in ensuring career growth and satisfaction.

References

1. Sweeney, L., & Williams, R. (2018). The Impact of Ergonomics on Workplace Productivity. *Journal of Occupational Health Psychology*.
2. American Psychological Association. (2020). The Impact of Light on Well-Being. Retrieved from https://www.apa.org
3. Gartner. (2021). Digital Collaboration Tools and Employee Engagement. Retrieved from https://www.gartner.com
4. Trello. (2021). How to Create a Productive Home Office. Retrieved from https://trello.com
5. GitHub. (2021). Remote Work. Retrieved from https://github.com/about

CHAPTER 4: EFFECTIVE COMMUNICATION ACROSS REMOTE TEAMS

In today's hybrid work landscape, effective communication is not just beneficial; it is essential for fostering collaboration, maintaining productivity, and ensuring that teams function smoothly despite geographical separation. The transition to remote and hybrid work models has transformed how teams communicate, collaborate, and build relationships. This chapter dives deep into the nuances of digital communication, strategies for building trust within virtual teams, and best practices for leading successful virtual meetings. Individuals and organizations can create a more cohesive and productive work environment by mastering these aspects.

Mastering Digital Communication

Digital communication serves as the lifeline for remote teams, connecting individuals who may be physically distant yet must collaborate effectively. With various platforms available, it is crucial to understand how to leverage these tools to enhance communication, clarify messages, and foster collaboration.

Email Communication

Email is often the primary mode of communication in professional settings. While it provides a convenient means to share information, it also has challenges. Misinterpretations can occur due to the absence of non-verbal cues, leading to misunderstandings. Here are strategies for effective email communication:

Craft Clear and Concise Messages:
Begin with a straightforward subject line that reflects the content. The first few lines summarize the main points, allowing readers to grasp the essence without wading through lengthy text. For instance, instead of "Meeting Request," specify "Request for Marketing Strategy Meeting on October 10." This clarity aids in prioritizing emails and reduces the chance of overlooked messages.

Use a Professional Tone:
Remember that written communication can be easily misconstrued. Maintain a professional tone and avoid slang or overly casual language that may detract from the message's seriousness. This is particularly important in diverse teams where cultural differences may influence interpretation.

Incorporate Actionable Steps:
 If your email requires the recipient to take specific actions, be explicit about these requirements. Use bullet points for clarity and indicate deadlines. For example, if you are assigning tasks, list them and specify who is responsible for what, along with due dates. This approach helps reduce back-and-forth clarifications and keeps everyone aligned.

Employ Email Etiquette:
Proper email etiquette includes timely responses and acknowledging receipt of important messages. This

demonstrates respect for your colleagues' time and reinforces a culture of accountability. For instance, if you receive a request that requires more time for a thorough response, consider sending a quick acknowledgment email stating that you are reviewing the information and will get back to them shortly.

Chat and Instant Messaging

With platforms like Slack, Microsoft Teams, and Google Chat becoming commonplace, instant messaging has revolutionized workplace communication. To use chat effectively:

Utilize Channels Appropriately:
Many messaging platforms allow you to create channels based on projects or teams. Use these channels to keep discussions organized. This helps avoid clutter in private messages and ensures that everyone involved in a project has access to relevant information.

Engage in Real-Time Conversations:
While emails can take time to receive responses, chat platforms enable real-time interactions. Utilize this feature to foster quick brainstorming sessions or seek immediate feedback on ideas. This can enhance collaboration and speed up decision-making processes.

Establish Guidelines:
Given chat's casual nature, setting guidelines on when to use it versus email is essential. For example, urgent queries that require immediate attention may warrant chat, while detailed discussions may be better suited for email. Establishing these norms can help teams navigate communication preferences and reduce frustration.

Leverage Emoji and GIFs Mindfully:
While emojis or GIFs can lighten the mood and foster camaraderie, you must gauge the appropriateness based on your team's culture. Consider the context of the conversation; what

might be suitable in a casual team setting may not resonate in a formal context. Finding the right balance is crucial for maintaining professionalism.

Video Calls

Video conferencing has become a vital aspect of remote work, facilitating face-to-face interactions that can help maintain personal connections. However, conducting effective virtual meetings requires thoughtful planning and execution:

Preparation is Key:

Before each meeting, prepare an agenda outlining the topics to be discussed and specific time allocations. Share this agenda with participants beforehand, allowing them to prepare adequately. This structured approach minimizes rambling and ensures that all critical points are addressed.

Engagement Techniques:

Keeping participants engaged during video calls can be challenging. To foster interaction, employ techniques such as asking open-ended questions, conducting polls, or using breakout rooms for smaller discussions. For example, during a team brainstorming session, you might divide participants into groups and assign each group a specific topic to discuss. Afterward, they can share their insights with the larger group.

Foster Inclusivity:

Ensure that all participants can contribute during the meeting. Actively invite input from quieter members or those hesitant to speak up. A simple question like, "Sarah, I would love to hear your thoughts on this," can encourage participation and create a more inclusive environment.

Follow-Up:

After the meeting concludes, send a summary of key points discussed, decisions made, and action items assigned. This reinforces accountability and ensures everyone is aligned on their responsibilities moving forward.

Building Trust Virtually

Establishing trust within remote teams is crucial for effective collaboration. Trust fosters open communication, encourages risk-taking, and creates a sense of belonging among team members.

Regular Check-Ins

Regular check-ins serve as a touchpoint to maintain connections among team members. These meetings can take various forms, including one-on-one sessions, team huddles, or informal catch-ups.

One-on-One Meetings:
These provide a safe space for employees to discuss their challenges, aspirations, and any feedback they may have. Managers can use this time to understand their employees' career goals and offer guidance or resources that align with those objectives.

Team Huddles:
Quick, informal meetings can help the team stay connected and focused on shared goals. For example, a marketing team might hold a weekly huddle to review campaign progress, celebrate achievements, and address any obstacles collectively.

Transparent Actions

Transparency in communication helps build trust and credibility. When employees feel informed about organizational decisions, they are more likely to trust their leaders and remain engaged in their work.

Share Company Updates:
Regularly communicate organizational changes, updates, and successes. Consider sending a monthly newsletter or hosting a town hall meeting to keep everyone informed.

Encourage Feedback:
Actively seek employee input regarding policies, processes, and initiatives. Create channels for anonymous feedback to ensure everyone feels comfortable sharing their thoughts.

Empathy in Communication

Fostering empathy within remote teams is essential for building solid relationships. Understanding the unique challenges faced by colleagues can create a more supportive environment.

Be Mindful of Individual Circumstances:
Remote work can present challenges beyond work responsibilities. A team member may be managing childcare, caring for elderly relatives, or coping with mental health issues. By acknowledging these realities, you can offer support and flexibility where needed.

Encourage Open Conversations:
Create an atmosphere where employees feel comfortable discussing personal challenges. Regularly check their well-being and offer resources such as mental health support or flexible scheduling options.

Leading Successful Virtual Meetings

Virtual meetings play a significant role in maintaining team cohesion and facilitating collaboration. To lead successful meetings, consider the following strategies:

Preparation
Preparation is essential for maximizing the effectiveness of virtual meetings. Leaders should:

Define Objectives: Clearly outline the purpose and goals of the meeting. Communicate these objectives in advance so participants can prepare and contribute meaningfully.

Create an Agenda: Develop a structured agenda with time allocations for each topic. Share the agenda beforehand to allow participants to prepare and gather necessary materials.

Test Technology: Before the meeting, ensure that all technology—video conferencing software, screen-sharing capabilities, and presentation tools—functions correctly. This minimizes technical difficulties during the conference.

Interaction

Engaging participants is crucial for productive meetings. Leaders should:

Encourage Participation: Use round-robin sharing or breakout rooms to promote participation. Ensure that all voices are heard, as this enhances collaboration and innovation.

Utilize Interactive Tools: Leverage tools such as polls, surveys, or shared documents to encourage real-time engagement. These tools can help gather feedback and facilitate discussions effectively.

Follow-Up

Following up after a meeting is critical to reinforce accountability and ensure that action items are addressed. Leaders should:

Summarize Key Points: After the meeting, send a recap that outlines major decisions, key takeaways, and assigned tasks. This summary keeps everyone informed and accountable.

Set Deadlines: Clearly outline deadlines for action items and follow up with team members as needed. This practice helps maintain momentum and encourages timely task completion.

Solicit Feedback: Encourage participants to provide feedback on the meeting's effectiveness. Understanding what worked and what could be improved helps enhance future meetings.

Effective communication is the foundation of successful remote teams. Individuals can enhance collaboration and productivity in a hybrid work environment by mastering digital communication, building trust, and leading engaging virtual meetings. As we move forward in this new work era, we must continue developing our communication skills and adapting to the changing work landscape.

References

1. Allen, N. J., & Meyer, J. P. (1990). The Measurement and Antecedents of Affective, Continuance, and Normative Commitment to the Organization. *Journal of Occupational Psychology*.
2. Harvard Business Review. (2020). How to Improve Virtual Meetings. Retrieved from https://hbr.org/2020/08/how-to-improve-virtual-meetings
3. MindTools. (n.d.). The Pomodoro Technique: How to Beat Procrastination and Get More Done. Retrieved from https://www.mindtools.com/pages/article/newTMC_1195.htm
4. University of California, Berkeley. (2021). Remote Work: Building Relationships in a Virtual Environment. Retrieved from https://hr.berkeley.edu
5. Google. (2021). The Future of Work: 5 Tips to Help You Transition to Remote Work. Retrieved from https://blog.google/products/working-remotely

CHAPTER 5: ACHIEVING WORK-LIFE BALANCE IN REMOTE WORK

The shift to remote work has fundamentally transformed how we approach our professional and personal lives. While the flexibility of working from home offers many advantages, it also presents unique challenges that can make maintaining a healthy work-life balance more difficult. This chapter will delve into the importance of defining boundaries, incorporating breaks and wellness routines, and recognizing the signs of burnout. We will provide actionable strategies to help individuals navigate the complexities of remote work, ensuring they can thrive professionally and personally.

Defining Boundaries

Establishing clear boundaries is essential for creating a healthy separation between work and personal life. In a remote work environment, where the lines can easily blur, having well-defined boundaries helps to mitigate stress and improve overall productivity (Miller, 2021). The concept of work-life balance is not merely about dividing time between work and personal activities; it is about ensuring that both areas are respected and can coexist harmoniously.

Setting Physical Boundaries

Establishing a dedicated workspace is one of the most effective ways to define boundaries. A physical space dedicated to work can signal to yourself and others when you are in "work mode." This separation can be crucial for mental clarity and focus.

For example, Jessica, a remote graphic designer, transformed a spare bedroom into her home office. By designing a workspace that inspired creativity—with plants, art, and good lighting—she boosted her productivity and created a physical distinction between her work and personal life (Smith, 2020). This commitment to creating a designated workspace not only helped Jessica maintain her focus during working hours but also allowed her to leave work behind at the end of the day, promoting a healthy separation between her professional and personal lives.

Creating a workspace that feels distinctly separate from personal areas can also help signal to other household members that work hours are in effect. For instance, using a specific chair or desk for work can create a mental trigger that signals, "I am working now," making it easier for you and your family to respect that time.

Communicating Availability

Effective communication about your availability is also critical. Letting family members, friends, and colleagues know your work hours can significantly minimize interruptions. Utilize digital calendars to mark off work hours and communicate these boundaries to your network.

For instance, Alex, a project manager, shared his work schedule with his family and colleagues. Using shared calendars, he set expectations regarding his availability for calls and social interactions, maintaining focus during work hours while ensuring quality time with loved ones during off-hours (Johnson, 2021). This proactive communication approach can help foster understanding and respect for boundaries, ultimately leading to a more balanced lifestyle.

Being transparent about your availability can also extend to setting expectations with your supervisor. For example, if you have specific periods when you will be unavailable due to family commitments, let your team know beforehand. This kind of clarity can minimize frustrations and help maintain team dynamics.

Digital Boundaries

In today's digital age, maintaining boundaries means being mindful of technology. The constant ping of notifications can be distracting and make focusing challenging. Implementing "do not disturb" settings on messaging apps or muting notifications outside of work hours can be effective strategies for managing these distractions.

For example, a remote software engineer, Nina, set her messaging app to "do not disturb" after 6 PM. She noticed a significant improvement in her evening relaxation and family time as she was no longer tempted to constantly check work messages or emails (Taylor, 2021). This small yet powerful adjustment enabled her to enjoy her time fully, knowing she could address work matters during designated hours.

Moreover, establishing specific technology-free zones within your home can further enhance your boundary-setting efforts. You are designating certain areas, such as the dining room or bedroom, as tech-free zones can foster a healthier work-life balance, allowing for family interaction and personal reflection without the interruptions of work-related devices.

Incorporating Breaks and Wellness

Amidst the demands of remote work, taking regular

breaks is vital for maintaining productivity and well-being. Incorporating wellness routines into your day can rejuvenate your mind and body, helping you stay focused and engaged (Davis, 2021). The importance of self-care cannot be overstated, especially in an environment where the boundary between work and home life is blurred.

The Importance of Regular Breaks

Research indicates that short, regular breaks can enhance productivity and creativity. The Pomodoro Technique, which involves working for 25 minutes followed by a 5-minute break, is a popular method that encourages this practice (Cirillo, 2018). This structured approach allows individuals to maintain their focus while ensuring they take the necessary time to recharge.

For instance, a content writer named Mark adopted the Pomodoro Technique and found that taking short breaks allowed him to recharge mentally. During these breaks, he would step away from his desk, stretch, or quickly walk around the block. This practice improved his focus and overall well-being (Adams, 2020). By making breaks a regular part of his work routine, Mark effectively enhanced his productivity and enjoyment of the workday.

Integrating Wellness Routines

Incorporating wellness routines into your daily schedule can significantly enhance your physical and mental well-being. This is crucial for maintaining productivity and a positive mindset, especially when working remotely. Wellness routines involve yoga, meditation, physical exercise, or simple daily stretches. Research shows regular physical activity can boost mood, improve concentration, and reduce stress levels (Biddle & Mutrie, 2008). Far from being a luxury, making time for wellness is necessary for anyone looking to sustain long-term remote work success.

Exploring Different Types of Wellness Routines

Yoga and Stretching:

Yoga is not only a physical exercise but also a mental one, promoting both flexibility and relaxation. Starting your day with a brief yoga session can set a positive tone, increasing alertness and reducing anxiety.

Even short stretching breaks throughout the workday can alleviate muscle stiffness, improve circulation, and prevent the physical strain often associated with prolonged sitting. Desk stretches, such as neck rolls, shoulder shrugs, and seated twists, can be performed regularly, helping maintain energy levels and focus.

Meditation and Mindfulness:

Meditation and mindfulness practices can be incorporated into your morning routine or used as a quick midday reset. Regular meditation helps reduce stress, enhance self-awareness, and increase overall well-being. Guided meditation apps like Headspace and Calm offer short sessions tailored to different needs, such as anxiety reduction, improved focus, or better sleep.

Mindfulness, which focuses on the present moment, can be practiced during daily activities like eating, walking, or working. For example, mindful eating during lunch—concentrating on your food's taste, texture, and aroma—can be a grounding practice that refreshes the mind for the remainder of the workday.

Physical Exercise:

Regular physical exercise, whether a brisk walk, a jog, or a home workout, is a proven way to boost mood and productivity. Studies indicate that moderate-intensity exercise can increase brain function, enhance memory, and improve problem-solving skills (Garcia, 2020).

Shortening sessions can be equally beneficial for those who struggle to find time for extended workouts. High-intensity interval training (HIIT), which involves short bursts of intense exercise followed by rest, can be a time-efficient way to maintain fitness and energy levels throughout the day. Many HIIT routines can be completed in 15-20 minutes, making them ideal for busy schedules.

Real-World Example: Emily's Wellness Journey
A marketing consultant, Emily prioritizes wellness as part of her remote work routine. She starts her day with a 15-minute yoga session followed by meditation. This routine helps her cultivate a sense of calm and clarity, setting a positive tone for her workday. Emily found that beginning the day with these activities enabled her to approach tasks with greater focus and a more positive mindset.

Midday Refreshment: **During her lunch break, Emily walked briskly, allowing her to clear her mind and return to work refreshed. This simple routine improved her mood and gave her energy that carried her through the afternoon.**

End-of-Day Stretching: **Emily performed a short stretching routine at the end of her workday to unwind and release accumulated tension. This helped her transition from work mode to personal time, reducing stress and promoting a better night's sleep.**

By prioritizing these wellness practices, Emily maintained her energy levels throughout the workday, improving her productivity and overall job satisfaction.

Engaging in Group Wellness Activities

Wellness routines do not have to be a solitary endeavor. Even virtually, group wellness activities can foster connection and promote accountability among remote colleagues. For example:

Virtual Exercise Classes:

Organizing virtual exercise classes, such as yoga, Pilates, or even dance sessions, can be a fun way for teams to stay active together. These sessions not only encourage physical fitness but also enhance team spirit and social interaction, creating a sense of camaraderie even in a remote setting.

Companies can schedule weekly wellness challenges, such as completing a set number of daily steps or attending a virtual fitness class. This adds an element of friendly competition, motivating participants to be consistent with their exercise routines.

Group Meditation Sessions:

Hosting virtual group meditation sessions can effectively promote mindfulness and stress reduction across the team. These sessions can be guided by a professional or facilitated through apps that offer group features.

Group meditation encourages a shared sense of calm and focus, which can improve communication, reduce stress, and increase overall job satisfaction among team members.

Virtual Running or Walking Clubs:

Forming a virtual running or walking club can be another great way to encourage wellness. Members can track their distances using fitness apps like Strava or MapMyRun, setting weekly goals and celebrating milestones together.

These clubs often incorporate social elements, such as virtual meetups where participants share their experiences, offer encouragement, and discuss how staying active has positively impacted their mental and physical well-being.

Wellness Workshops and Seminars:
Companies can host virtual workshops or seminars on wellness topics like nutrition, stress management, or ergonomic workspaces. These events provide valuable information and practical tips that can be implemented immediately, enhancing employees' overall quality of life.

Wellness experts can be invited to speak about "Healthy Eating Habits for Remote Workers" or "Managing Stress through Mindfulness," offering insights and strategies that resonate with remote employees.

Overcoming Challenges in Maintaining Wellness Routines

While integrating wellness routines into a remote workday can be highly beneficial, it can also present challenges, such as time constraints, lack of motivation, or difficulty establishing a consistent routine. Here are some strategies to overcome these challenges:

Start Small:
Begin by incorporating short, manageable wellness activities into your day. Even a 5-minute meditation or a quick stretch can make a difference. As these small routines become habits, you can gradually increase the duration and variety of activities.

Use Technology for Accountability:
Apps like Habitica or Streaks can help you set wellness goals and track progress. These tools offer reminders and rewards for consistency, helping you stay accountable to your wellness routines.

Sharing your progress with a colleague or a friend can also motivate you. Virtual check-ins, where you discuss your wellness achievements and challenges, can be a helpful way to maintain commitment and receive encouragement.

Schedule Wellness Breaks:
Block specific times in your calendar for wellness activities, just as you would for meetings or work tasks. Treating wellness as a non-negotiable part of your schedule ensures that it receives the attention it deserves.

If possible, align wellness breaks with your natural energy rhythms. For example, schedule a quick walk or a stretching session during your afternoon slump to re-energize for the rest of the day.

Create a Dedicated Space for Wellness:
Set up a small area in your home dedicated to wellness activities. Having a designated space for yoga, meditation, or stretching can create a mental association that reinforces your commitment to wellness.

Prioritizing Mental Health

Prioritizing mental health is as critical as managing physical well-being in remote work. The flexibility of working from home can bring unique challenges, such as feelings of isolation, increased stress, or difficulty setting boundaries between work and personal life. Recognizing the signs of stress or burnout and taking proactive steps to manage them is essential. Remote workers can maintain productivity, job satisfaction, and well-being by addressing mental health needs.

Understanding Mental Health Challenges in Remote Work

Identifying Signs of Stress and Burnout:
Remote workers can experience signs of stress and burnout, including fatigue, irritability, reduced concentration, and a sense of detachment from work. These symptoms can emerge when boundaries between work and personal life are blurred, leading to overworking and mental exhaustion.

Proactively identifying these signs is the first step toward managing mental health effectively. Regular self-assessment—such as reflecting on energy levels, mood, and motivation—can help remote workers recognize when they need a break or when stress escalates.

Creating Work-Life Boundaries:
Setting clear boundaries between work and personal time is crucial for mental well-being. Remote workers can establish these boundaries by designating a specific workspace, setting defined work hours, and using "do not disturb" features during off-hours. By mentally and physically separating work from personal life, remote workers can prevent work from encroaching on downtime.

Communicating these boundaries to colleagues and supervisors is equally essential, ensuring that expectations align with personal well-being. For instance, turning off work notifications during evenings or weekends can help create a sense of closure at the end of the workday.

Personal Strategies for Enhancing Mental Health

Mindfulness Practices:
Mindfulness practices, such as meditation or deep-breathing exercises, can be practical tools for managing stress. Mindfulness encourages focusing on the present moment, reducing anxiety about past mistakes or future uncertainties. Apps like Headspace, Insight Timer, and Calm offer guided meditations designed for stress reduction and mental clarity.
Practicing mindfulness for 5-10 minutes each morning or during breaks can create a sense of calm, improve focus, and help reset the mind during demanding tasks. Incorporating these short sessions into a daily routine can significantly improve mental resilience (Kabat-Zinn, 1990).

Journaling for Mental Clarity:

Journaling can be a robust mental health tool. It allows individuals to process their thoughts, reflect on daily experiences, and identify patterns contributing to stress or anxiety. Writing down thoughts and feelings can provide insights into emotional triggers, helping remote workers understand and address specific stressors.

For example, after feeling overwhelmed during a busy project, John, a software developer, started journaling his thoughts and feelings. This practice helped him process his emotions, identify stressors, and gain clarity on how to manage his workload more effectively (Wells, 2021). By integrating journaling into his routine, John cultivated resilience and fostered a healthier approach to work.

Seeking Professional Support:
Remote workers may sometimes benefit from professional mental health support, such as therapy or counseling. Virtual therapy sessions offer convenient access to mental health professionals, allowing individuals to discuss their challenges and receive guidance on managing stress, anxiety, or work-life balance.

Many therapists now specialize in remote work-related stress, helping clients navigate the unique demands of working from home. Remote workers can also explore support groups or online mental health forums to share experiences and coping strategies with peers facing similar challenges.

Incorporating Relaxation Techniques:
Relaxation techniques, such as progressive muscle relaxation, guided imagery, or even listening to calming music, can help reduce stress and improve overall mental well-being. These activities can be used as quick breaks during the workday or as part of a winding-down routine at the end of the day.
Some remote workers find it helpful to schedule regular "mental health breaks," stepping away from their screens, engaging in a

relaxing activity, or resting in a quiet space. These breaks can prevent burnout and help maintain mental sharpness.

Organizational Initiatives for Promoting Mental Health

Organizations play a crucial role in supporting the mental well-being of remote employees. Companies can create a more supportive and productive work environment by implementing mental health initiatives.

Offering Mental Health Days:
Just as employees are given sick days for physical illnesses, companies can introduce mental health days to encourage workers to take time off when they are feeling mentally overwhelmed. Mental health days allow employees to recharge without the pressure of providing a reason, helping to normalize mental well-being as an integral part of overall health.

When organizations openly support mental health days, employees are more likely to use them without fear of stigma, creating a healthier work culture.

Access to Counseling Services:
Providing access to counseling or Employee Assistance Programs (EAPs) can be a valuable resource for remote workers. EAPs often offer confidential counseling, mental health assessments, and crisis support, providing employees with the tools they need to manage stress and emotional challenges.
Some organizations also partner with mental health platforms, like Talkspace or BetterHelp, to offer discounted virtual therapy options to remote workers or as part of their benefits package.

Workshops and Seminars on Mental Health:
Hosting workshops and seminars on mental health topics, such as stress management, building resilience, or coping with remote work challenges, can educate employees on practical strategies for maintaining well-being. These sessions can be

led by mental health professionals and tailored to address the specific needs of remote workers.

Topics like "Managing Anxiety During Uncertain Times" or "Building Resilience in Remote Work" can offer employees actionable insights and coping mechanisms, empowering them to handle stress more effectively.

Building a Supportive Culture:
Creating an open and supportive culture around mental health is essential for remote teams. Managers and team leaders should encourage conversations about mental health and check in regularly with team members to ensure they manage their workload and stress levels well.

Promoting a culture of vulnerability—where employees feel safe to express when they are struggling—can help build trust and reduce the stigma associated with mental health discussions. When employees feel heard and supported, they are more likely to engage positively with their work and contribute to a healthier team dynamic.

Regular Well-Being Check-Ins:
In addition to work-related meetings, organizations can implement regular well-being check-ins, where employees are encouraged to share their feelings and what support they might need. These check-ins can be informal, such as virtual coffee chats, or structured, using anonymous surveys to gather insights about employees' mental health.

Managers can also use one-on-one meetings to discuss mental health openly, showing empathy and offering flexible solutions, such as adjusted workloads or extended deadlines when needed.

Strategies for Sustaining Long-Term Mental Health

To sustain mental health over the long term, remote workers

should consider developing a comprehensive mental wellness plan that integrates personal strategies and organizational support:

Build Consistent Routines:
Establishing consistent daily routines can provide structure and stability, reducing feelings of unpredictability that often contribute to stress. This includes setting regular wake-up and sleep times, maintaining consistent meal schedules, and designating specific work hours.

Incorporating wellness activities—like exercise, meditation, or a hobby—into the daily routine can create a balanced approach to work and personal life.

Connect Socially:
Social connections are vital for mental health. Remote workers should make an effort to engage with colleagues, friends, or family, even if it is through virtual channels. Socializing can offer emotional support, reduce feelings of isolation, and provide a mental break from work-related stress.

Virtual team-building activities, like online games or collaborative projects, can also strengthen relationships and boost morale, fostering a sense of belonging among remote employees.

Practice Gratitude:
Practicing gratitude can positively impact mental health by shifting focus from stressors to positive aspects of life. Maintaining a gratitude journal, where individuals write down things they are thankful for daily, can increase feelings of happiness and resilience.

Incorporating gratitude into team culture—such as sharing appreciation for colleagues during meetings or in messages—can enhance team dynamics and contribute to a more positive remote work environment.

Prioritizing mental health is essential to thriving in a remote work environment. Remote workers can manage stress effectively and maintain overall well-being by integrating personal mental wellness strategies, such as mindfulness, journaling, and professional support, alongside organizational initiatives like mental health days, counseling services, and a supportive culture. A commitment to mental health enhances individual productivity and job satisfaction and fosters a healthier, more resilient work culture for everyone involved.

Avoiding Burnout in Remote Work

Burnout is a natural and pressing concern in remote work environments. The lack of physical separation between work and personal life and increased expectations for availability can contribute to burnout over time. Recognizing its signs and implementing strategies to avoid it is crucial for long-term sustainability, well-being, and job satisfaction.

Understanding Burnout

Burnout is a state of physical, emotional, and mental exhaustion caused by prolonged stress or excessive workload. It can affect motivation, performance, and overall mental health. In remote work settings, where boundaries between work and home are often blurred, burnout can develop insidiously, gradually impacting personal and professional life.

Recognizing Signs of Burnout

Burnout manifests in various ways, including chronic fatigue, decreased motivation, and feelings of isolation. It is essential to be aware of these signs and take proactive measures before burnout worsens. Here are some common indicators:

Emotional Exhaustion:
> Emotional exhaustion is characterized by feeling drained or overwhelmed by your workload. It often involves a sense of fatigue that does not improve with rest or relaxation. For remote workers, this might present as dreading the start of the workday, feeling mentally "checked out," or lacking the

emotional energy to engage with tasks and colleagues.

Early signs include irritability, trouble focusing, and feeling "on edge." Individuals might find themselves quickly frustrated by minor inconveniences or making more errors in tasks they previously managed well.

Reduced Performance and Productivity:

Burnout can lead to a noticeable decline in productivity or the quality of work. Once manageable tasks feel daunting, remote workers might need help completing them within standard time frames.

There may also be a lack of enthusiasm or motivation to excel, resulting in a "just get it done" approach to tasks. Deadlines may be missed, and creativity or problem-solving skills may decline as mental energy wanes.

Detachment and Cynicism:

Developing a sense of cynicism or detachment from work responsibilities is a common symptom of burnout. Individuals may feel disconnected from their tasks, colleagues, or the organization's mission. For remote workers, this can manifest as feeling isolated, disengaged during virtual meetings, or indifferent about achieving team goals.

Detachment might also involve a loss of passion for work, a decreased sense of personal achievement, or increased doubt about one's professional capabilities (Maslach & Leiter, 2016).

Recognizing these symptoms early allows individuals to take proactive steps to address their mental health before reaching a point of crisis. Regular self-checks, open communication with supervisors, and maintaining a supportive network can help identify burnout in its early stages.

Implementing Strategies for Balance and Prevention

To combat burnout, it is essential to implement sustainable strategies that promote a healthy work-life balance. Here are some detailed approaches to help prevent and manage burnout:

Set Realistic Goals and Prioritize Tasks:

Establishing realistic goals helps manage workload expectations and reduce feelings of overwhelm. Break larger projects into smaller, manageable tasks that can be achieved step-by-step. This approach maintains a sense of progress and provides opportunities to celebrate small victories, boosting motivation.

Use techniques like the SMART criteria—Specific, Measurable, Achievable, Relevant, and Time-bound—to set clear, attainable objectives. For instance, instead of aiming to "finish the entire project this week," set a goal to "complete the first draft of the report by Wednesday."

Implement tools like task management apps (e.g., Trello, Asana) to organize tasks visually, prioritize urgent tasks, and track progress. Seeing tasks checked off a list can provide a psychological boost, reinforcing a sense of accomplishment (Locke & Latham, 2002).

Limit Work Hours and Establish Boundaries:

Establish precise work hours and stick to them consistently. Designate a firm start and end time for your workday, and communicate this boundary to colleagues and supervisors. This can prevent the workday from creeping into personal time, which is crucial for mental recovery.

Use technology to reinforce these boundaries. Set "do not disturb" hours in communication tools like Slack or Microsoft Teams to minimize after-hours messages and notifications. Setting up automated "out of office" replies outside work hours can signal unavailability and help maintain boundaries.
Create a physical boundary within your home, such as a dedicated workspace, to mentally separate work from personal

life. Having a distinct area for work helps reinforce the end of the workday when you leave that space, reducing the temptation to "just check one more email" during downtime.

Engage in Social and Community Activities:

Make time for social interactions, whether virtual or in-person. Regular engagement with friends, family, or colleagues can combat feelings of isolation, provide emotional support, and boost overall well-being. Even casual conversations can serve as a mental reset, helping individuals feel more connected and valued.

Organize virtual social events like game nights, coffee breaks, or themed team activities to foster colleague connections. Virtual social gatherings can help replicate the camaraderie of in-person work environments, creating a more supportive and inclusive atmosphere.

Participate in community groups, hobbies, or volunteer activities outside of work. Engaging in non-work-related activities that bring joy and fulfillment can counterbalance work stress and provide a sense of purpose beyond professional achievements (Kahn, 2017).

Incorporate Regular Breaks and Downtime:

Incorporate short breaks throughout the workday to maintain energy levels and prevent mental fatigue. Techniques like the Pomodoro method (25 minutes of focused work followed by a 5-minute break) can help structure work sessions and encourage regular breaks.

Schedule longer breaks, such as lunch hours away from the desk, to ensure a mental reset during the day. Stepping outside, engaging in light exercise, or practicing a quick meditation can boost mood and productivity for the remainder of the day.

Use downtime to engage in relaxing activities that promote

well-being, such as reading, listening to music, or practicing a hobby. Regularly dedicating time to enjoyable activities can prevent the monotony of remote work from setting in.

Take Time Off to Recharge:

Do not hesitate to use vacation, personal, or mental health days. Time off helps prevent burnout by allowing for full psychological and physical recovery. Short breaks, such as a long weekend, can significantly improve energy levels and motivation.

Plan regular time away from work, even if it is a staycation, to step back from responsibilities and recharge. Disconnecting from work-related emails and tasks during this time is crucial to ensure a complete break and renewal.

To maintain balance, consider "micro-breaks" throughout the year—such as half-days off or extended lunch breaks. Micro-breaks can provide quick but impactful rest periods, helping sustain energy and prevent prolonged fatigue.

Focus on Physical and Mental Wellness:

Incorporate wellness activities like exercise, meditation, or deep breathing exercises into daily routines. Regular physical activity reduces stress, boosts energy, and improves overall mental health. Aim for at least 30 minutes of moderate exercise most days of the week.

Practice mindfulness or meditation to manage stress and maintain mental clarity. Just a few minutes of mindfulness daily can reduce anxiety, improve focus, and enhance emotional resilience—apps like Headspace or Calm offer guided meditation sessions tailored to stress management and mental recovery.

Seek Support and Professional Help When Needed:

Communication with supervisors or HR about workload, stress levels, or difficulties managing work expectations can be beneficial. Requesting additional support or workload adjustments is often necessary to prevent burnout.

If burnout symptoms persist, consider seeking professional help, such as therapy or counseling. Many remote workers find that talking to a mental health professional effectively manages stress, improves coping skills, and maintains mental well-being.

Use Ergonomics to Enhance Comfort:

Ensuring a comfortable workspace can reduce physical strain and mental fatigue. Invest in ergonomic furniture, like an adjustable chair or a standing desk, to maintain good posture and relieve physical discomfort during long hours of remote work.

Incorporate visual and auditory comfort into the workspace, such as adjusting lighting to reduce eye strain and using noise-canceling headphones to minimize distractions. Creating a pleasant work environment can enhance focus, reduce stress, and improve overall job satisfaction.

Avoiding burnout in remote work requires a proactive approach, balancing personal well-being with professional responsibilities. Remote workers can maintain long-term mental and physical health by recognizing the early signs of burnout and implementing strategies like setting boundaries, incorporating breaks, engaging socially, and prioritizing wellness. Embracing these preventive measures enhances productivity and job satisfaction and fosters a sustainable and fulfilling remote work experience.

Creating a Supportive Environment

Fostering a supportive work culture is essential for preventing burnout within teams. Employers should encourage open conversations about workload and well-being, creating an environment where employees feel comfortable discussing their challenges (Demerouti et al., 2001).

For example, during a company-wide meeting, the CEO of a tech startup encouraged employees to share their struggles with remote work and brainstorm solutions together. This initiative fostered a culture of transparency and support, allowing employees to feel more connected and less isolated.

Achieving work-life balance in a remote work environment requires intentional effort and strategic planning. By defining boundaries, incorporating wellness routines, and recognizing signs of burnout, individuals can cultivate a healthier and more sustainable approach to their work. As we continue navigating this evolving landscape, prioritizing balance will be essential for maintaining productivity, satisfaction, and overall well-being.

In the subsequent chapters, we will explore additional strategies for enhancing productivity, fostering teamwork, and maintaining mental health in remote and hybrid settings. Together, we can create a thriving work environment that supports professional growth and personal fulfillment.

References

1. Adams, S. (2020). *The Impact of Short Breaks on Productivity.* Harvard Business Review.
2. Biddle, S. J. H., & Mutrie, N. (2008). *Psychology of Physical Activity: Determinants, Well-Being and Interventions.* Routledge.
3. Cirillo, F. (2018). *The Pomodoro Technique: The Acclaimed Time-Management System That Has Transformed How We Work.* Crown Publishing Group.
4. Davis, L. (2021). *The Importance of Regular Breaks in the Workplace.* Journal of Occupational Health Psychology.
5. Demerouti, E., Bakker, A. B., & Gevers, J. M. (2001). The role of self-regulation in work-life balance: A longitudinal study. *Journal of Occupational Health Psychology*, 6(3), 205–218.
6. Garcia, M. (2020). *Morning Routines: The Impact of Yoga and Meditation on Productivity.* Mindful Magazine.

7. Kahn, W. A. (2017). *The Social Psychology of the Workplace: A Socioecological Perspective.* Psychology Press.
8. Kabat-Zinn, J. (1990). *Whole Catastrophe Living: Using the Wisdom of Your Body and Mind to Face Stress, Pain, and Illness.* Delta.
9. Locke, E. A., & Latham, G. P. (2002). Building a practical theory of goal setting and task motivation: A 35-year odyssey. *American Psychologist*, 57(9), 705–717.
10. Maslach, C., & Leiter, M. P. (2016). *Burnout and Engagement in the Workplace: A Review of the Literature.* Annual Review of Organizational Psychology and Organizational Behavior, 3, 29–52.
11. Miller, R. (2021). *The New Remote Work Culture: Navigating Challenges and Opportunities.* Forbes.
12. Smith, J. (2020). *Creating a Productive Home Office: Tips for Remote Workers.* Remote Work Journal.
13. Taylor, P. (2021). *Setting Boundaries in Remote Work: Strategies for Success.* Business Insider.
14. Wells, A. (2021). *The Role of Journaling in Mental Health and Well-Being.* Psychology Today.

CHAPTER 6: NAVIGATING CAREER GROWTH FROM AFAR

Navigating Career Advancement in a Remote Work Environment

In today's rapidly evolving job market, the shift to remote work has created unique opportunities for professionals looking to advance their careers. While traditional pathways to promotion and professional development have often relied on in-person interactions, remote work demands new strategies for growth. With a proactive approach, individuals can successfully seek promotions, build leadership roles, upskill, and network from anywhere. This chapter will delve into comprehensive strategies for advancing careers remotely, emphasizing the importance of visibility, skill development, and digital networking.

Advancing Remotely: Strategies for Seeking Promotions and Leadership Roles

Advancing your career while working remotely requires a strategic mindset and a clear action plan. It is not just about excelling in your current role but also about positioning yourself for new opportunities. Here is how to seek promotions and leadership roles effectively, even from a distance:

1. Communicate Your Ambitions Clearly and Consistently

One of the most significant challenges of remote work is the lack of visibility that employees may experience. Ensuring that your supervisors and team leaders know your career goals and aspirations is essential without regular face-to-face interactions. Here are specific steps to communicate effectively:

Schedule Regular One-on-One Meetings: Be sure to express your ambitions before annual performance reviews. Proactively schedule monthly or quarterly check-ins with your manager to discuss your progress, goals, and interest in taking on more responsibility. Use these meetings to review your achievements, share ideas, and ask for feedback.

> *Example*: Sarah, a project coordinator at a tech company, initiated monthly check-ins with her manager. During these meetings, she communicated her interest in advancing to a project manager role, shared her progress, and asked for guidance on improving her skills. As a result, her manager began assigning her to lead more minor projects, enabling her to gain experience and visibility within the organization (Miller, 2021).

Be Transparent About Your Goals: Clearly articulate your desire for promotion or leadership roles, specifying what roles or projects interest you. For example, if you aspire to move from a marketing analyst to a marketing manager role, express your interest in leading campaigns or managing a team.

> *Example*: Tom, a customer support representative, communicated his ambition to transition to a training manager role. By expressing his interest and sharing a plan to upskill in relevant areas (like customer service training programs), he positioned himself for internal opportunities when they became available (Davis, 2021).

Leverage Performance Metrics: Use data to demonstrate your contributions and readiness for promotion. Track key performance indicators (KPIs) that show your impact, such as increased sales, improved customer satisfaction, or cost savings. Presenting tangible results in discussions with your manager strengthens your case for promotion.

2. Demonstrate Initiative and Leadership from Afar

In a remote setting, demonstrating initiative is vital for standing out and positioning yourself as a valuable asset. Taking proactive steps to contribute beyond your current role enhances your visibility and shows your readiness for leadership. Here is how to do it:

Volunteer for Special Projects: Look for opportunities to lead or contribute to special projects that align with organizational goals. This could include leading a new product launch, organizing a virtual event, or heading a task force for process improvements.

> *Example*: Mark, a remote marketing specialist, noticed that his team struggled with coordination during a challenging project. He volunteered to coordinate weekly team meetings, improving team communication and highlighting his organizational skills. His proactive approach led to a promotion to a team lead position (Smith, 2020).

Mentor New Employees: Offer to mentor new employees or junior team members. This demonstrates your commitment to the team's success and positions you as a leader, even without a formal title.

> *Example*: Emma, a remote HR specialist, started mentoring new hires on company processes and best practices. Her guidance improved onboarding and showcased her leadership potential, resulting in a promotion to HR manager (Johnson, 2021).

Propose Process Improvements: Identify areas where workflows or processes can be optimized and suggest improvements. Support your suggestions with data, research, or case studies demonstrating potential benefits like cost savings, efficiency gains, or better team collaboration.

> *Example*: Kelly, a remote operations manager, noticed inefficiencies in her team's communication processes. She researched and proposed a new project management tool, presenting a clear plan for its implementation. The successful rollout improved productivity and boosted her credibility as a problem-solver (Taylor, 2021).

3. Seek Continuous Feedback and Adapt

Regularly seeking feedback is crucial for personal and professional growth. It helps you identify strengths, weaknesses, and areas for improvement, allowing you to refine your skills and adapt to evolving expectations. Here is how to establish a feedback-driven growth mindset:

Create a Feedback Loop: After completing projects or tasks, ask colleagues and managers for feedback on your performance. This demonstrates your willingness to learn and improve, an attractive quality for leadership roles.

> *Example*: After completing a significant marketing campaign, Kelly, a remote graphic designer, asked her team for feedback on her designs and overall performance. The constructive criticism helped her refine her skills and build stronger relationships with her team members (Johnson, 2021).

Request Constructive Criticism in One-on-One: During regular meetings with your manager, actively request feedback on specific projects or skills. Use this feedback to develop an action plan for growth, outlining steps to address weaknesses or gaps.

> *Example*: Jake, a software engineer, asked his manager

for feedback after each project sprint, focusing on code quality, teamwork, and communication. This continuous feedback helped him improve, and he was promoted to lead developer (Garcia, 2020).

Use Self-Assessment Tools: In addition to external feedback, conduct regular self-assessments to reflect on your performance. Tools like SWOT analysis (Strengths, Weaknesses, Opportunities, and Threats) can help you evaluate your growth areas and set clear development goals.

Upskilling for Remote Careers: Building Critical Skills for Advancement

As remote work transforms industries, upskilling is essential for career advancement. Professionals must identify and pursue skills that are in demand for remote roles. Here are detailed strategies to enhance your skill set and remain competitive:

1. Identify Critical Skills for Remote Success

Researching and identifying the skills in demand within your industry is the first step to upskilling effectively. Here is how to approach this process:

Analyze Job Postings: Review job postings for roles you aspire to, noting recurring skills and qualifications. Consider emerging abilities like digital communication, data analysis, remote project management, and leadership.

> *Example*: After noticing a surge in demand for data analysis skills, Emma, a remote business analyst, enrolled in an online data analytics course. This proactive step broadened her skill set and positioned her as a competitive candidate for promotion (Davis, 2021).

Consult Industry Reports: Look for industry reports, white papers, or career guides highlighting skill trends. Resources like LinkedIn's Emerging Jobs Report or the World Economic Forum's

Future of Jobs Report provide insights into high-demand skills, enabling you to align your learning with market needs.

Seek Guidance from Mentors: Mentors or senior colleagues can offer valuable insights into skills critical for career growth. Ask for recommendations on courses, certifications, or areas of focus that align with your career goals.

2. Leverage Online Learning Platforms for Continuous Growth

Online learning platforms offer a convenient way to develop new skills and earn certifications that boost your qualifications. Here is how to make the most of these resources:

Enroll in Relevant Courses: Websites like Coursera, LinkedIn Learning, Udemy, and edX offer a wide range of courses on digital marketing, project management, and leadership. Choose classes that align with your career goals and provide certificates upon completion.

> *Example*: Jake, a software developer, completed a series of courses on agile project management through LinkedIn Learning. He earned certifications and demonstrated his expertise and readiness for organizational leadership roles (Garcia, 2020).

Pursue Professional Certifications: Certifications like PMP (Project et al.), Google Analytics, or Six Sigma can significantly enhance your resume and demonstrate your commitment to professional growth. Research which certifications are most valuable in your field and invest in them to boost your credibility.

Participate in Webinars and Virtual Workshops: Webinars and virtual workshops offer insights into industry trends and best practices. They provide opportunities for continuous learning while expanding your professional network.

> *Example*: During webinars on digital marketing trends,

Linda, a remote marketer, connected with professionals from other companies. These connections provided valuable insights and potential collaborations, enhancing her career prospects (Adams, 2020).

Networking in the Digital Age: Building Relationships Virtually

Networking remains vital to career growth, even in a remote setting. Building professional relationships digitally requires a strategic approach, leveraging online platforms and virtual events. Here is how to network effectively in the digital age:

1. Optimize Your LinkedIn Profile for Visibility

LinkedIn is a powerful tool for networking and building your professional brand. To maximize its potential, follow these steps:

Complete and Optimize Your Profile: Ensure your LinkedIn profile is current and reflects your skills, experience, and career aspirations. Use a professional profile photo, craft a compelling headline, and write a detailed summary highlighting your achievements and goals.

Engage Actively with Your Network: Share relevant content, comment on industry posts, and join discussions in LinkedIn groups. Actively participating in conversations enhances your visibility and positions you as a thought leader in your field.

> For example, a recent college graduate, Mark, used LinkedIn to connect with alums working in his desired field. By engaging in discussions and sharing insights, he expanded his professional network and gained valuable career advice (Miller, 2021).

2. Participate in Virtual Conferences and Meetups

Virtual conferences and meetups offer excellent opportunities for networking, learning, and career growth. Here is how to make the most of these events:

Attend Sessions Aligned with Your Goals: Choose sessions that match your career interests and actively participate in discussions. Ask questions during Q&A segments, engage with speakers, and use chat features to connect with attendees.

> *Example*: During a virtual tech conference, Jennifer attended sessions on artificial intelligence and actively contributed to discussions. Her engagement expanded her knowledge and helped her connect with industry leaders (Smith, 2020).

Join Online Professional Groups: Platforms like Meetup.com, Eventbrite, and industry-specific LinkedIn groups offer opportunities to join virtual meetups. Engaging in these communities fosters meaningful connections and opens doors for collaborations or mentorship.

3. Utilize Virtual Coffee Chats for Personalized Networking

Virtual coffee chats are a valuable way to build relationships in a more personal setting. Here is how to approach them:

Request Informational Interviews: Contact professionals in your field for informational interviews. Be specific about what you hope to learn and how much time you request (e.g., 20-30 minutes).

> *Example*: David, a freelance writer, used LinkedIn to connect with experienced writers and request virtual coffee chats. These conversations provided career insights and led to collaborations and freelance opportunities (Taylor, 2021).

Follow Up and Maintain Connections: After a virtual coffee chat, follow up with a thank-you email and mention specific points from the conversation. Regularly check in with contacts to maintain relationships and share updates on your progress.

Navigating career growth in a remote work environment requires proactive strategies and a willingness to adapt. By effectively seeking promotions, upskilling, and leveraging digital networking opportunities, individuals can position themselves for success. As remote work evolves, embracing these strategies will enhance professional development and contribute to a fulfilling and rewarding career.

In the following chapters, we will explore additional strategies for thriving in the remote and hybrid workplace, helping you unlock your full potential.

References
1. Adams, S. (2020). *The Impact of Short Breaks on Productivity.* Harvard Business Review.
2. Davis, L. (2021). *The Importance of Regular Breaks in the Workplace.* Journal of Occupational Health Psychology.
3. Garcia, M. (2020). *Morning Routines: The Impact of Yoga and Meditation on Productivity.* Mindful Magazine.
4. Johnson, A. (2021). *Building Your Professional Brand Online: Strategies for Success on LinkedIn.* Career Development Quarterly.
5. Kahn, W. A. (2017). *The Social Psychology of the Workplace: A Socioecological Perspective.* Psychology Press.
6. Miller, R. (2021). *The New Remote Work Culture: Navigating Challenges and Opportunities.* Forbes.
7. Smith, J. (2020). *Creating a Productive Home Office: Tips for Remote Workers.* Remote Work Journal.
8. Taylor, P. (2021). *Setting Boundaries in Remote Work: Strategies for Success.* Business Insider.

CHAPTER 7: LEADING REMOTE AND DISTRIBUTED TEAMS

The shift to remote and distributed work models has transformed the landscape of team leadership. As companies adapt to this new norm, leaders must develop effective strategies to manage teams across different locations, time zones, and cultures. This chapter will explore remote leadership strategies, how to create a remote-friendly culture, and the need to adapt performance review processes for remote teams. By understanding and implementing these strategies, leaders can foster collaboration, accountability, and a sense of belonging among their team members.

Remote Leadership Strategies

Leading remote teams presents unique challenges that require thoughtful strategies to ensure success. Here are several critical approaches to effective remote leadership:

Establishing Clear Expectations for Remote Team Success

Setting clear expectations is fundamental to managing remote teams effectively. In a virtual environment, where face-to-face interactions are limited, clarity becomes even more crucial to ensure alignment, accountability, and productivity. Remote teams can experience confusion, miscommunication, and decreased motivation without clear expectations. Leaders must communicate goals, deadlines, and performance metrics transparently to maintain cohesion and drive results. Here is how to establish clear expectations and foster a productive remote team environment.

Critical Strategies for Setting Clear Expectations

1. Communicate Goals and Objectives Clearly

Define Team and Individual Goals: Start by setting clear, measurable, and achievable goals for both the team as a whole and individual members. Use the SMART criteria (Specific, Measurable, Achievable, Relevant, Time-bound) to ensure that goals are well-defined and provide a clear roadmap for success. For example, instead of saying "increase sales," specify, "increase sales by 10% within the next quarter through targeted marketing campaigns."

Break down larger organizational objectives into smaller, actionable tasks that each team member can contribute to. This approach clarifies the team's direction and helps individuals understand how their work aligns with broader goals.

Create a Centralized Document for Goals: Utilize shared documents or project management tools to maintain a centralized source of goals and objectives. Platforms like Google Docs, Asana, or Monday.com can outline goals, key performance indicators (KPIs), and timelines. This shared document serves as a reference point for all team members, providing visibility into expectations and progress.

Provide Context for Goals: Communicate the "why" behind each goal to enhance motivation and engagement. Explain how achieving these objectives contributes to the team's success, mission, and individual growth. This context helps team members see the bigger picture and understand the value of their work.

2. Outline Clear Roles and Responsibilities

Create Detailed Job Descriptions: Each team member should clearly understand their role, duties, and scope of work. Develop detailed job descriptions that outline responsibilities, critical tasks, and reporting lines. This clarity helps team members know what is expected of them and prevents role overlaps.

For example, if a team includes a content strategist, a writer, and a social media manager, ensure that each role is distinctly defined. The content strategist might focus on planning and overseeing campaigns, the writer on creating content, and the social media manager on distribution and engagement.

Use Role-Specific KPIs: Establish role-specific KPIs that provide measurable outcomes for each position. For example, a customer service representative might have KPIs related to response time, customer satisfaction scores, and resolution rates. In contrast, a marketing specialist could have KPIs focused on lead generation, conversion rates, and campaign effectiveness.

Review these KPIs regularly during one-on-one meetings to discuss performance, challenges, and growth opportunities. Adjust KPIs as needed to reflect changing priorities or organizational needs.

Document Responsibilities in Project Management Tools: Use tools like Trello, Asana, or Basecamp to assign tasks, set due dates, and monitor progress. Documenting responsibilities in a shared platform allows team members to quickly understand their roles, track tasks, and visualize the workflow.

Example: A marketing team might use Asana to assign tasks related to a new campaign, set deadlines for content drafts, and track the progress of each deliverable. By providing visibility into individual roles and responsibilities, leaders can ensure that everyone knows what is expected of them and how their contributions impact the project's success.

3. Implement Regular Check-Ins and Progress Reviews

Conduct Weekly or Bi-Weekly Team Meetings: Regular team meetings are essential for discussing progress, addressing challenges, and aligning priorities. These meetings provide an opportunity to review tasks, update the team on project status, and clarify expectations. Use a standardized agenda to keep meetings focused and efficient, covering critical areas like goal updates, blockers, and next steps.

Encourage team members to share updates on their progress, voice concerns, or suggest plan adjustments. This open communication fosters transparency and ensures everyone is on the same page.

Host One-on-One Check-Ins: Hold regular one-on-one check-ins with individual team members in addition to team meetings. These meetings provide a platform for more personalized feedback, support, and discussion of individual goals. Use this time to review progress toward KPIs, address any challenges, and offer personal and professional development guidance.

Example: During a one-on-one, a manager might discuss a team member's progress on a project, offer feedback on recent work, and provide tips for overcoming specific obstacles. This direct interaction helps maintain alignment and reinforces individual expectations.

Provide Regular Performance Feedback: Offer constructive feedback regularly, not just during annual reviews. Use performance data, such as metrics from project management tools or customer feedback, to provide specific insights into how healthy team members are meeting expectations. Consistent feedback helps individuals understand their performance, adjust their approach, and stay aligned with goals.

4. Develop a Comprehensive Onboarding Process

Create an Onboarding Document: Develop a detailed onboarding document for new team members that outlines the team's goals, KPIs, timelines, and communication protocols. This document should also include an overview of the team's structure, roles, and current projects, providing new hires with a comprehensive understanding of expectations from day one.

Incorporate links to essential documents, project management tools, and communication channels, making it easy for new team members to access crucial resources. This approach accelerates the onboarding process and helps new employees acclimate quickly.

Assign a Mentor or Buddy: Pair new team members with an experienced colleague who can act as a mentor or "buddy" during onboarding. This mentorship helps new hires understand expectations, navigate team dynamics, and ask questions in a more informal setting.

Set Clear Milestones for New Hires: Establish milestones for new team members during their first 30, 60, and 90 days. These milestones should align with their role's KPIs and provide measurable outcomes for assessing progress. For example, a new sales representative might be expected to complete product training within 30 days, make their first sales call by day 60, and achieve a specific sales target by day 90.

5. Utilize Effective Communication Channels

Choose the Right Communication Tools: Different communication tools serve different purposes. For example, use Slack or Microsoft Teams for quick messages, Zoom for video calls and meetings, and email for more formal communications. Ensure team members understand when to use each channel and establish response times and availability protocols.

Example: A product development team might use Slack for day-to-day communication, Asana for task management, and Zoom for weekly sprint meetings. By clarifying which tools to use for specific types of communication, leaders can reduce confusion and improve response times.

Establish Communication Norms: Establish explicit communication norms, such as expected response times, preferred channels for urgent issues, and guidelines for virtual meetings (e.g., turning cameras on during team discussions). Document these norms in a communication guide that is accessible to all team members.

For instance, if immediate responses are needed, team members should know to use direct messaging on Slack rather than sending an email. This clarity ensures efficient communication and reduces decision-making delays.

6. Track Progress and Adjust Expectations as Needed

Use Dashboards to Track Progress: Implement dashboards or visual trackers that provide real-time updates on progress toward goals and KPIs. Tools like Tableau, Jira, or HubSpot offer dashboards that allow team members to see where projects stand and how their contributions impact overall performance.

Review these dashboards regularly during team meetings to discuss what is working, identify roadblocks, and adjust priorities. Visual progress tracking keeps everyone informed and aligned with team objectives.

Adapt Expectations to Changing Circumstances: In a remote work environment, circumstances can change rapidly, whether due to shifting priorities, new projects, or external factors. Be prepared to adjust expectations accordingly. Communicate any changes clearly and promptly, explaining how they impact goals, roles, or timelines.

For example, if a new client project requires immediate attention, clarify how it will affect current projects and what adjustments need to be made. Transparency in adapting expectations helps maintain trust and flexibility within the team.

Example: Effective Implementation in a Marketing Team
Consider a remote marketing team working on a product launch. To establish clear expectations, the team leader uses the following approach:

- **Tools**: The leader utilizes tools like Asana for task management, Slack for communication, and Zoom for weekly meetings.
- **Onboarding Document**: New hires receive an onboarding document that outlines the project's goals, timelines, KPIs, and communication protocols.
- **Task Assignment**: Tasks are assigned in Asana, with detailed descriptions, deadlines, and listed responsible individuals.
- **Progress Reviews**: Weekly team meetings review task progress, address challenges, and adjust priorities based on updated client requirements.
- **Role Clarity**: The leader sets clear KPIs for each role, such as "generate 1,000 leads by the end of the campaign" for the lead generation specialist and "increase social media engagement by 20%" for the social media manager.

This structured approach fosters accountability, reduces confusion, and ensures all team members understand their roles, responsibilities, and the overall project objectives.

Fostering Open Communication in Remote Teams

Open communication is a cornerstone of successful remote teams. Creating a transparent and collaborative environment is essential for maintaining engagement, alignment, and trust among team members without in-person interactions. Effective communication ensures tasks are completed efficiently and fosters a positive team culture where individuals feel heard and valued. Leaders play a critical role in establishing and maintaining this open dialogue. Here is how to foster open communication within remote teams and encourage a culture of transparency and engagement.

Strategies for Building Open Communication

1. Create a Culture of Psychological Safety

Encourage Openness and Vulnerability: Psychological safety is the foundation of open communication. Team members should feel comfortable sharing ideas, concerns, and feedback without fear of judgment or retribution. Encourage openness by modeling vulnerability as a leader—share your challenges, admit mistakes, and invite constructive criticism.

Example: During team meetings, leaders can share recent learning experiences, such as acknowledging a project misstep and discussing how it was resolved. This approach normalizes open discussions about challenges and encourages team members to express their concerns or seek help.

Celebrate Diverse Perspectives: Actively encourage diverse viewpoints by inviting input from all team members during meetings or brainstorming sessions. Use phrases like, "I would love to hear your thoughts" or "What do you think about this approach?" to ensure everyone has a voice. Recognizing and valuing diverse perspectives improves decision-making and promotes a sense of belonging and engagement.

2. Implement Regular Check-Ins and Team Meetings

Schedule Frequent Team Check-Ins: Regular team check-ins are essential for keeping everyone aligned and informed in remote settings. Weekly or bi-weekly meetings allow for updates on progress, discussion of roadblocks, and real-time feedback. Make these meetings interactive by inviting team members to share their updates, ask questions, and propose ideas.

Use a standard agenda that includes time for open discussions. Encourage team members to raise concerns or suggest adjustments to projects. This structure not only enhances clarity but also builds trust and collaboration.

Host Daily Stand-Up Meetings for Agile Teams: For agile teams, daily virtual stand-up meetings can be an effective way to maintain momentum. These brief meetings (typically 10-15 minutes) allow team members to share what they worked on yesterday, what they plan to work on today, and any challenges they face. This format promotes accountability, ensures visibility, and facilitates quick problem-solving.

Example: Dropbox implemented regular virtual stand-up meetings to keep team members connected and engaged (Davis, 2020). These meetings foster a sense of community and collaboration by allowing employees to share progress, discuss roadblocks, and celebrate achievements in a structured yet informal manner.

Offer One-on-One Meetings: Besides team check-ins, regular one-on-one meetings between leaders and team members are vital for personal development and well-being. Use these sessions to discuss performance, address concerns, and provide individualized feedback. This personal touch helps build trust and encourages open communication.

Leaders should ask open-ended questions like, "What challenges are you currently facing?" or "How can I better support you?" to encourage honest conversations and identify areas for improvement.

3. Encourage the Use of Multiple Communication Channels

Diversify Communication Tools: Different team members may have different communication preferences. By providing a variety of communication channels—such as instant messaging (e.g., Slack, Microsoft Teams), video calls (e.g., Zoom, Google Meet), and email—leaders can cater to these preferences, ensuring that all team members have access to tools they feel comfortable using.

Instant messaging can be more efficient for quick questions or updates, while video calls may be better suited for detailed discussions or brainstorming sessions. Email can be used for formal communications, such as reports or project documentation. Encourage team members to use the appropriate channel based on the nature of the communication.

Set Clear Communication Norms: Establish clear guidelines for communication, such as response times, preferred channels for urgent matters, and expectations for meeting participation (e.g., turning cameras on during team meetings). Document these norms in a communication guide that is accessible to all team members.

Example: In a product development team, the communication guide might specify that Slack should be used for day-to-day updates, Zoom for weekly team meetings, and email for more extended reports. By defining these norms, leaders can streamline communication and ensure team members know how and when to reach out.

4. Promote Informal Communication and Team Bonding
Organize Virtual Social Events: To foster a sense of camaraderie, organize virtual social events such as virtual coffee breaks, online game sessions, or themed "happy hours." These informal gatherings allow team members to connect personally, building stronger relationships and reducing feelings of isolation.

Example: During a virtual coffee break, team members might share stories about their weekend, discuss hobbies, or celebrate personal milestones. This informal communication strengthens team bonds and contributes to a more cohesive and supportive team culture.

Create Dedicated Channels for Non-Work-Related Conversations: Use messaging platforms like Slack or Microsoft Teams to create channels specifically for casual chats. Channels like "#random" or "#watercooler" allow team members to share memes, discuss TV shows, or chat about non-work topics.

Encourage participation in these channels by sharing fun prompts or questions, such as "What is your favorite weekend activity?" or "Share a picture of your pet." These interactions foster community and make remote teams feel more connected.

Establish "Open Hours" for Casual Conversations: Leaders can create "open hours" where team members can drop in for informal chats. These open hours can be scheduled once or twice a week, allowing team members to have casual conversations with their manager or peers, similar to spontaneous in-office chats.

Example: A manager might set aside an hour on Wednesday afternoons for open office hours, where team members can join a Zoom call to ask questions, discuss projects, or chat about non-work topics. This approach promotes a friendly and approachable atmosphere.

5. Model Effective Communication as a Leader

Be Approachable and Responsive: Leaders should model effective communication by being approachable, responsive, and open to feedback. When team members see leaders actively engaging and encouraging dialogue, they are more likely to feel comfortable sharing their thoughts and concerns.

Respond to messages promptly, actively listen during meetings, and use inclusive language to make team members feel valued. For example, acknowledge individual contributions during a meeting by saying, "That is a great point, Jane—thank you for sharing your perspective."

Provide Clear and Consistent Updates: Keep the team informed about organizational changes, project updates, and progress toward goals. Consistent updates help maintain transparency and trust, reducing uncertainty and speculation within the team.

Example: A project manager might send a weekly summary email with updates on project status, upcoming milestones, and any priority changes. This transparency ensures everyone is on the same page and helps team members understand how their efforts contribute to overall success.

Encourage Feedback Loops: Invite feedback from team members regularly, whether about projects, processes, or leadership style. Use surveys, anonymous feedback forms, or direct conversations to gather insights. Showing that you value feedback and act on it helps create a culture of continuous improvement and open communication.

Example: A leader might ask for feedback on its effectiveness after implementing a new communication tool. If team members express challenges with the tool, the leader should address these concerns promptly, making necessary adjustments.

6. Address Communication Barriers Proactively

Identify and Resolve Communication Challenges: Be proactive in identifying and addressing communication barriers, such as language differences, time zone challenges, or technical issues. Use asynchronous communication tools, like recorded video messages or project management updates, to bridge time zone gaps.
For multilingual teams, consider offering language support or using tools that facilitate translation. Additionally, use shared documents or asynchronous communication to ensure important updates are accessible to all team members,

regardless of time zone.

Adapt to Different Communication Styles: Team members may have different communication styles; some prefer direct communication, while others are more reserved. As a leader, be aware of these differences and adapt your approach to encourage everyone's participation.

For example, introverted team members might feel more comfortable sharing ideas in written form rather than speaking up in a video call. To ensure all voices are heard, provide opportunities for written feedback, such as in Google Docs comments or Slack threads.

Example: Effective Implementation at Dropbox
Dropbox, a well-known tech company, has implemented regular virtual stand-up meetings to keep team members connected and engaged (Davis, 2020). These brief daily or weekly meetings allow employees to share progress, discuss roadblocks, and celebrate achievements. In addition to structured meetings, Dropbox encourages informal communication through virtual coffee breaks and dedicated Slack channels for non-work-related chats. This combination of formal and informal communication fosters a sense of community, reduces isolation, and promotes collaboration among team members.

Building Trust and Accountability in Remote Teams

Trust is the foundation of any successful team, and it becomes even more critical in a remote environment where physical distance can create barriers to communication and connection. Building trust requires intentional efforts from leaders and team members alike in the absence of in-person interactions. Trust fosters collaboration, increases engagement, and drives performance. In tandem with trust, accountability ensures that team members meet expectations and deliver results consistently. Here is how to establish trust and responsibility in a remote setting while maintaining a culture of mutual respect and transparency.

Strategies for Building Trust in Remote Teams

1. Empower Autonomy and Decision-Making

Delegate Responsibility Clearly: One of the most effective ways to build trust is to empower team members with autonomy. Delegate tasks and projects, allowing individuals to take ownership of their work. Giving team members the authority to decide their roles fosters trust and confidence.

Instead of micromanaging, offer guidance and support when needed, but allow team members to approach tasks in their own way. This approach shows trust in their abilities and encourages innovation and initiative.

Encourage Independent Problem-Solving: Promote a culture where team members feel empowered to solve problems independently before seeking help. While support should always be available, encouraging team members to develop their problem-solving skills builds confidence and trust within the team.

Example: A project manager might encourage a junior developer to propose solutions for a technical issue before escalating it to senior developers. This practice builds trust and fosters professional growth by allowing team members to learn from their experiences.

Provide Decision-Making Opportunities: Trust grows when team members are given opportunities to make decisions that impact projects or processes. Involve team members in strategic discussions, ask for their input on critical decisions, and empower them to implement changes that align with team goals.

For instance, a marketing team could empower a social media

specialist to decide on campaign themes, content formats, and promotional strategies. By trusting the specialist's expertise, the team leader builds trust and encourages a sense of ownership.

2. Establish Transparent Communication and Accountability

Promote Transparency with Open Communication: Open communication is essential for building trust. Leaders should be transparent about decisions, changes, and the rationale behind strategic moves. Regular updates, team meetings, and progress reports keep everyone informed and foster a culture of transparency.

Example: At GitLab, a remote software development team relies heavily on asynchronous communication and transparency to build trust. Team members openly share project updates, code reviews, and documentation, enabling everyone to stay informed and engaged (Garcia, 2021). This openness promotes trust by allowing team members to understand what others are working on and how their roles fit into the larger picture.

Use Public Tracking Tools for Accountability: Implement tools like Asana, Trello, or Jira, where tasks, deadlines, and project updates are visible to all team members. This transparency enhances accountability and helps team members understand each other's workloads and priorities.

For example, suppose a project manager uses Trello to track task assignments and progress. In that case, team members can easily see who is responsible for each task, which is overdue, and how projects are progressing. This visibility encourages accountability and ensures that team members meet their commitments.

Conduct Regular Performance Reviews: Schedule regular performance reviews, both formal and informal, to discuss progress, set goals, and provide feedback. These reviews create opportunities to recognize achievements, address challenges, and establish accountability for future performance.

During performance reviews, use metrics and data to provide objective feedback. For instance, a sales manager might review metrics like sales targets, conversion rates, and customer feedback to assess a sales representative's performance. Constructive feedback helps reinforce accountability while providing a clear path for improvement.

3. Implement Peer Feedback Mechanisms

Encourage Peer Reviews and Feedback: Establish a system where team members can provide feedback to each other regularly. Peer feedback mechanisms can include structured peer reviews, 360-degree feedback sessions, or informal check-ins.

For example, a development team might conduct code reviews, in which developers evaluate each other's work, offering constructive criticism and suggestions for improvement. This enhances accountability and fosters collaboration and knowledge sharing within the team.

Normalize Constructive Criticism: For peer feedback to be effective, it is essential to create a culture where constructive criticism is seen as an opportunity for growth rather than personal criticism. Encourage team members to focus on specific behaviors or outcomes rather than making personal judgments.

Train team members on how to give and receive feedback constructively, using techniques like "I" statements (e.g., "I noticed that..." or "I think it would be helpful if..."). This approach helps prevent misunderstandings and promotes a culture of continuous improvement.

Use Feedback Tools for Anonymity: In situations where anonymity is needed to foster honest feedback, consider using tools like SurveyMonkey, Typeform, or Officevibe to gather feedback anonymously. This can help team members feel more comfortable sharing candid feedback, especially in the early stages of building trust.

4. Celebrate Contributions and Recognize Achievements

Acknowledge Individual and Team Successes: Regularly celebrate individual and team achievements to build a culture of appreciation. Recognition can be given during team meetings, through shout-outs in messaging channels, or even with rewards like digital gift cards or certificates.

For example, a customer support manager might recognize a representative who consistently achieves high customer satisfaction ratings by mentioning their success in a team meeting or sending a personalized thank-you email. This recognition reinforces the importance of accountability while building morale and trust.

Highlight Contributions Publicly: Use project management tools or team dashboards to highlight completed tasks, milestones achieved, or exceptional performance. Publicly acknowledging contributions builds trust and motivates team members to continue performing well.

Consider regularly implementing a "Team Member of the Month" program or a "Recognition Wall" in the team's communication platform to celebrate outstanding efforts and contributions.

Share Success Stories: Stories of successful projects, collaborations, or problem-solving efforts within the team. Highlighting these stories boosts morale and demonstrates the positive outcomes of trust and accountability in action.

For instance, a product development team might share the story of a successful product launch, recognizing the efforts of the design, marketing, and development teams. This storytelling approach fosters a sense of pride and reinforces trust within the team.

5. Cultivate Psychological Safety for Open Dialogue

Create a Safe Space for Risk-Taking: Psychological safety is essential for trust, as it encourages team members to take risks, share ideas, and express concerns without fear of judgment or negative consequences. Leaders can foster psychological safety by actively inviting input, responding positively to suggestions, and treating mistakes as learning opportunities.

Example: A project manager might say, "Let us treat this as an experiment—if it works, great; if not, we will learn from it." This approach encourages team members to innovate and share ideas openly, knowing their contributions are valued.

Encourage Vulnerability from Leaders: Leaders play a crucial role in setting the tone for openness and vulnerability. By sharing personal stories, admitting mistakes, and seeking feedback, leaders can model vulnerability and create an environment where team members feel comfortable sharing their thoughts and concerns.

For instance, a leader might say during a team meeting, "I made an error in the last project timeline, and I appreciate the team's flexibility in adapting to the changes. Let us work together to improve our planning for the next project." This openness from leaders sets a precedent for trust and honesty.

Respond Constructively to Mistakes: When team members make mistakes, respond with support and a focus on learning rather than punishment. Encourage a growth mindset by discussing what can be learned from the error and how similar issues can be prevented in the future.

For example, if a team member misses a deadline due to a miscommunication, discuss the factors that led to the delay and work together to improve communication processes. This constructive approach reinforces trust and accountability while fostering a culture of learning.

Maintain Consistent Follow-Through
Deliver on Promises: Trust is built through consistent follow-through. Leaders should ensure they deliver on promises and commitments, whether related to providing feedback, offering resources, or addressing concerns from team members.

If a leader commits to providing additional training or addressing workload issues, it is essential to take concrete action. Consistent follow-through demonstrates reliability and strengthens trust within the team.

Use Accountability Checkpoints: Establish regular accountability checkpoints where progress toward goals and commitments is reviewed. These checkpoints can be part of weekly team meetings, individual check-ins, or formal performance reviews.

During these checkpoints, discuss what is working well, what challenges exist, and what adjustments must be made. This regular review process reinforces accountability and ensures team members stay aligned with expectations.

Example: Trust and Accountability at GitLab
GitLab, a fully remote software development company, exemplifies trust and accountability by focusing on asynchronous communication, transparency, and peer feedback (Garcia, 2021). By sharing project updates, code reviews, and documentation openly, GitLab fosters a culture where team members can hold each other accountable while working collaboratively. Using open channels for feedback, regular performance reviews, and recognition of contributions further enhances trust within the team. GitLab's emphasis on psychological safety encourages team members to take risks, share ideas, and innovate, ultimately leading to a more engaged and productive workforce.

Building trust and accountability in remote teams requires

intentional strategies that promote autonomy, transparency, feedback, and recognition. Leaders can create a mutual respect and reliability culture by empowering team members, encouraging open dialogue, and maintaining consistent follow-through. Trust and accountability enhance individual and team performance and foster a positive work environment where team members feel valued, engaged, and committed to shared goals.

Creating a Remote-Friendly Culture

Building and maintaining a strong company culture in a remote environment can be challenging but is essential for employee engagement and retention. Here are some strategies for cultivating a remote-friendly culture:

Onboarding for Success in Remote Teams

A well-structured onboarding process is crucial for integrating new employees into the company culture and setting them up for long-term success. In a remote environment, where in-person interactions are limited, the onboarding process must be thoughtfully designed to ensure new hires feel welcomed, included, and supported. Effective remote onboarding goes beyond technical training; it helps new employees understand the company's values, fosters meaningful connections, and provides the tools needed to thrive in their roles. Here is how to create a successful remote onboarding program that promotes engagement and a sense of belonging from day one.

Critical Components of Effective Remote Onboarding

1. Start with Pre-Onboarding Preparation

Send a Welcome Kit Before Day One: The onboarding process should start even before the new hire's first day. Send a welcome kit with a personalized welcome letter, company swag (e.g., branded T-shirts, notebooks, or mugs), and an outline of what to expect during the first week. This gesture creates excitement and helps new employees feel valued from the beginning.

Include a list of essential tools, login credentials, and links to necessary resources, such as the company's intranet, onboarding documents, and training materials. This proactive approach helps new hires feel prepared and reduces first-day anxiety.

Assign Onboarding Buddy: Pair new employees with an onboarding buddy—an experienced team member who can provide guidance, answer questions, and offer informal support during the initial weeks. The buddy system helps new hires navigate the company culture, processes, and tools more comfortably, creating a personal connection that fosters a sense of belonging.

Example: At Buffer, a social media management company, new hires are paired with onboarding buddies who guide them through their first 90 days. The buddy helps answer questions about company culture, work processes, and even social norms within the team, making the onboarding process smoother and more engaging (Smith, 2020).

2. Facilitate Virtual Introductions and Team Building

Host a Virtual Welcome Meeting: On the new hire's first day, host a virtual welcome meeting with their team members, manager, and key colleagues. This initial meeting should be informal, focusing on introductions, team roles, and a general overview of the company's mission and values. Video conferencing tools like Zoom or Microsoft Teams can facilitate face-to-face interactions, even from a distance.

Encourage team members to share personal fun facts, hobbies, or recent achievements to create a relaxed atmosphere. This helps break the ice and makes new hires feel more connected to the team.

Organize Virtual Team Lunches or Coffee Breaks: During the first week of onboarding, organize virtual team lunches or coffee breaks to foster informal connections. These sessions allow new hires to get to know their colleagues in a relaxed setting, promoting camaraderie and a sense of inclusion.

Example: Zoom, a company known for its remote collaboration tools, has developed a comprehensive onboarding program that includes virtual team lunches and welcome videos from executives. These activities help new hires acclimate to the company culture and build relationships from the start (Johnson, 2020).

Use Interactive Onboarding Tools: Incorporate interactive tools like Slack channels for new hires, virtual whiteboards (e.g., Miro, MURAL), and icebreaker activities to engage new employees. Create a dedicated onboarding Slack channel where new hires can introduce themselves, ask questions, and interact with other newcomers. This channel serves as a hub for onboarding discussions and support.

3. Provide Comprehensive Training on Tools and Processes

Develop a Detailed Onboarding Plan: Create a structured onboarding plan that outlines the training sessions, resources, and milestones for the first 30, 60, and 90 days. Include a checklist that covers essential tools (e.g., Slack, project management software), processes (e.g., communication protocols), and job-specific skills. This roadmap gives new hires a clear understanding of what to expect and helps them track their progress.

For example, a software development company might create an onboarding plan that includes training sessions on version control tools (e.g., GitHub), coding standards, and internal workflows. New hires can hit the ground running by setting clear expectations and providing relevant resources.

Offer Interactive Training Sessions: Conduct live, virtual training sessions that allow new hires to ask questions in real-time and engage with trainers. Use screen-sharing tools, breakout rooms, and Q&A segments to make training more interactive and practical.

In addition to live training, offer recorded training sessions that new hires can revisit at their own pace. This flexibility accommodates different learning styles and time zones, ensuring all new employees receive the information they need to succeed.

Provide Access to an Online Knowledge Base: Ensure new hires access an online knowledge base or learning management system (LMS) containing detailed information about the company's tools, processes, and best practices. This resource should be easily navigable and have sections dedicated to different departments, roles, and training materials.

Example: HubSpot, a marketing software company, offers new hires access to an extensive online knowledge base that includes tutorials, FAQs, and how-to guides. This centralized resource allows new employees to find answers to their questions quickly and independently (Taylor, 2021).

4. Incorporate Regular Check-Ins and Feedback Sessions

Schedule Frequent Check-Ins with Managers: During the initial weeks of onboarding, managers should schedule regular one-on-one check-ins with new hires. These check-ins provide a platform for discussing progress, addressing concerns, and offering feedback. Regular check-ins also create opportunities to adjust training plans based on the new hire's input and needs.

Use these sessions to ask open-ended questions like, "How are you finding the onboarding process so far?" or "Is there anything we can do to make your transition smoother?" This proactive approach ensures that new hires feel supported and valued.

Gather Feedback on the Onboarding Experience: Through surveys or informal discussions, solicit feedback from new hires about their onboarding experience. Ask for input on what worked well, what could be improved, and whether they feel adequately prepared for their role.

Use feedback to refine the onboarding process continuously, adjusting training content, timelines, or communication methods as needed. This iterative approach improves the onboarding experience for future hires and demonstrates a commitment to growth and improvement.

Set Short-Term Goals and Milestones: Establish short-term goals for new hires, such as completing a specific training module within the first week or participating in a team project within the first month. These goals help new employees build confidence and gain a sense of accomplishment as they progress through onboarding.

Review these goals regularly during check-ins to track progress and make any necessary adjustments. This approach provides new hires with a clear path for growth and a sense of purpose from the beginning.

5. Integrate Company Culture and Values

Share the Company's Mission and Values: From day one, emphasize the company's mission, values, and culture. Incorporate these elements into onboarding materials, welcome presentations, and training sessions to help new hires understand how their role contributes to the organization's overall purpose.

Use real-life examples and stories to illustrate how the company's values are implemented. For instance, if one of the company's values is "innovation," share a success story of how a team's innovative solution led to a positive outcome.

Host Virtual Culture Workshops: Organize virtual workshops or sessions on the company's culture, values, and history. These workshops can be led by HR representatives, senior leaders, or even long-term employees who can share personal stories about their experiences at the company.

Use interactive activities like polls, quizzes, and breakout discussions to engage new hires and memorably reinforce cultural values. For example, a workshop might include a quiz on company values, followed by a discussion on how those values are reflected in everyday work.

Create Opportunities for Cross-Departmental Interactions: Encourage new hires to connect with colleagues from different departments through virtual "get-to-know-you" sessions or cross-departmental project involvement. This approach broadens new employees' understanding of the company's operations and helps them build a more comprehensive network of connections.

For instance, a new hire in marketing might have a virtual coffee chat with a sales representative to learn more about the sales process and how marketing materials support sales efforts.

6. Enhance Engagement with Mentorship Programs

Establish Formal Mentorship Programs: Pair new hires with mentors who can provide guidance, share insights, and help them navigate the company's culture and processes. A structured mentorship program offers new hires a trusted resource for questions, feedback, and career advice.

Mentors should schedule regular meetings with new hires to discuss their progress, offer feedback, and provide support. These sessions can be more informal than manager check-ins and focus on personal growth, career development, and work-life balance.

Encourage Informal Networking Opportunities: In addition to formal mentorship, create opportunities for informal networking. This could include virtual meetups, lunch-and-learns, or "ask me anything" (AMA) sessions with senior leaders. These events allow new hires to learn from different perspectives and engage with colleagues beyond their immediate team.

For example, LinkedIn, a professional networking platform, hosts virtual AMA sessions where new hires can ask executives and senior leaders questions. This approach promotes transparency and helps new employees feel more connected to the organization's leadership (Garcia, 2021).

Example: Remote Onboarding at Zoom

Zoom, a leading company in remote collaboration, has developed a comprehensive onboarding program that includes virtual team lunches, welcome videos from executives, and access to an online knowledge base. This approach helps new hires acclimate to the company while fostering a sense of belonging (Johnson, 2020). Zoom also uses a buddy system, where new employees are paired with experienced team members who provide guidance and support during the initial weeks. Regular check-ins with managers and mentors ensure new hires receive ongoing feedback and support throughout their transition.

Effective remote onboarding involves more than just training—it involves creating a welcoming environment that makes new hires feel included, valued, and supported. By incorporating virtual introductions, detailed training, regular check-ins, and cultural integration, organizations can set new employees up for success from day one. A robust onboarding process enhances employee engagement and lays the foundation for long-term productivity and retention in a remote work environment.

Recognition and Appreciation

Recognizing employee achievements and contributions is crucial for fostering a positive remote culture. Leaders should implement regular recognition programs to celebrate individual and team successes, such as monthly awards or shout-outs in team meetings. This acknowledgment helps employees feel valued and motivated.

For example, Buffer has a peer recognition program where employees can nominate colleagues for recognition in monthly team meetings. This practice boosts morale, reinforces the company's values, and encourages collaboration (Adams, 2021). Regularly highlighting accomplishments in team newsletters or company-wide emails can also serve as a reminder of the collective efforts and successes.

Additionally, leveraging platforms like Bonusly or Kudos can facilitate real-time recognition among peers, allowing team members to give and receive appreciation for their contributions. These platforms often enable employees to redeem points for rewards, further enhancing motivation and engagement.

Engage Through Virtual Team-Building Activities

Regular virtual team-building activities, such as online games and quizzes, virtual coffee breaks, and team challenges, can help strengthen relationships among remote team members. Leaders can foster camaraderie and trust within the team by creating opportunities for informal interactions.

A case in point is HubSpot, which organizes monthly virtual happy hours where employees can socialize, share experiences, and engage in fun activities. These gatherings contribute to a sense of community and help maintain team cohesion (Miller, 2021). Implementing themed team-building events like trivia nights or cooking classes can keep engagement levels high and promote a friendly atmosphere.

Moreover, incorporating wellness activities, such as virtual yoga sessions or mindfulness workshops, can help employees relieve stress and foster a sense of well-being. Encouraging team members to share personal interests or hobbies during meetings can create bonding opportunities and foster a supportive environment.

Adapting Performance Reviews for Remote Teams

Performance reviews are critical to employee development but require adaptation in remote work settings. Here are vital considerations for adjusting evaluation processes for remote teams:

Focus on Outcomes and Impact

In remote work environments, evaluating employees based on outcomes and impact is essential rather than solely on hours worked or visibility. Leaders should assess how well employees meet their goals, contribute to team projects, and support the organization's objectives. Setting clear performance metrics aligned with company goals will provide a framework for evaluation.

For instance, Microsoft has shifted its performance evaluation approach to prioritize results and team collaboration rather than individual metrics alone. This change emphasizes the importance of teamwork and the collective success of remote teams (Taylor, 2020). By incorporating 360-degree feedback, leaders can gain insights from peers, subordinates, and supervisors to paint a comprehensive picture of an employee's performance.

Use Technology for Continuous Feedback

Leveraging technology can enhance the performance review process by enabling continuous feedback. Platforms like 15Five or Lattice allow managers and team members to give and receive real-time feedback, creating a culture of ongoing development rather than waiting for annual reviews.

By encouraging regular check-ins and feedback exchanges, organizations can foster a growth mindset and help employees adjust their performance throughout the year. This approach aligns with the idea that feedback should be timely and constructive, contributing to continuous improvement (Kahn, 2017). For example, weekly or bi-weekly feedback sessions can give employees actionable insights to continuously refine their skills and performance.

Incorporate Employee Self-Assessments

Encouraging employees to participate in their performance evaluations through self-assessments can lead to a more comprehensive review process. By reflecting on their achievements and areas for improvement, employees can engage in meaningful conversations with their managers about their performance and career development.

For instance, Google's engineering team uses self-assessments for its performance review process. This practice allows employees to take ownership of their development and fosters open dialogue with managers about career aspirations (Garcia, 2021). Implementing self-assessment questionnaires before formal reviews can facilitate more in-depth discussions during performance meetings.

Additionally, training on conducting self-assessments effectively can empower employees to evaluate their performance critically and set actionable goals for their development. This process encourages a proactive approach to career growth and fosters a culture of continuous improvement.

References

1. Adams, S. (2021). *Peer Recognition Programs: Boosting Employee Morale in Remote Teams.* Remote Work Journal.
2. Davis, L. (2020). *Creating Community in a Remote*

Work Environment: Best Practices for Managers. Harvard Business Review.

3. Garcia, M. (2021). *Building Trust in Remote Teams: Strategies for Success.* Forbes.
4. Johnson, A. (2020). *Onboarding in a Remote World: Integrating New Employees into Your Culture.* SHRM.
5. Kahn, W. A. (2017). *The Social Psychology of the Workplace: A Socioecological Perspective.* Psychology Press.
6. Miller, R. (2021). *The New Remote Work Culture: Navigating Challenges and Opportunities.* Business Insider.
7. Smith, J. (2021). *Effective Communication in Remote Teams: Strategies for Success.* Remote Work Journal.
8. Taylor, P. (2020). *Performance Evaluations in Remote Work: Adapting to New Norms.* Journal of Business Psychology.

CHAPTER 8: STAYING AHEAD OF REMOTE WORK TRENDS

As remote work redefines the professional landscape, employees and organizations must stay ahead of emerging trends. Understanding and adapting to these changes can significantly enhance productivity, employee satisfaction, and overall organizational success. This chapter will delve into the rise of digital nomadism, the future of remote work, and strategies for adapting to the evolving work environment.

Embracing Digital Nomadism

Digital nomadism has gained immense popularity in recent years, mainly driven by technological advances and the flexibility of remote work. Digital nomads leverage technology to work remotely while traveling or living in various locations. This lifestyle combines work and travel, creating unique personal and professional growth opportunities. As more companies adopt flexible work policies, the digital nomad lifestyle becomes increasingly accessible to a broader audience.

The Appeal of Digital Nomadism

For many, the allure of becoming a digital nomad lies in the freedom to choose where to live and work. This lifestyle offers numerous benefits, such as exploring new cultures, meeting diverse people, and experiencing different ways of life. According to a study by the International Workplace Group (IWG), 70% of professionals would choose to work remotely at least once a week if given the option, indicating a significant shift in how people view traditional office work (IWG, 2020).

Exploring the Benefits of Digital Nomadism

Geographic Freedom:
The primary appeal of digital nomadism is the freedom to work from anywhere in the world. This geographic flexibility allows individuals to tailor their work environment to suit their preferences, whether a beachside café in Thailand, a co-working space in Berlin, or a mountain cabin in Colorado.

Nomads can also follow ideal weather patterns, moving to warmer climates during winter or cooler regions in summer. This adaptability enhances the quality of life and boosts mental well-being, as individuals can enjoy environments that support their happiness.

Improved Work-Life Balance:
Digital nomadism allows individuals to break free from the constraints of the typical 9-to-5 work schedule and office environment. This newfound flexibility can improve work-life balance, increase job satisfaction, and enhance well-being.

Many digital nomads report heightened productivity when working in inspiring locations, surrounded by new experiences and scenery that fuel creativity. For example, working from a café overlooking the Mediterranean Sea might provide a refreshing change of pace that enhances focus and motivation.

Cultural Immersion:
One of the most enriching aspects of digital nomadism is the opportunity to immerse oneself in different cultures. Nomads can learn new languages, participate in local customs, and engage with diverse communities. This exposure to other perspectives often leads to personal growth, increased empathy,

and a more global outlook on life and work.

By engaging with locals, digital nomads gain insights into cultural nuances that can enhance their professional interactions. Understanding the communication styles of different cultures can be beneficial in global business dealings, as it allows for more effective collaboration.

Networking Opportunities:

Digital nomadism facilitates global networking. By joining co-working spaces, attending local meetups, and engaging in digital nomad communities, individuals can build a diverse network of professional contacts from various industries and regions.

Platforms like Meetup and Nomad List host events specifically designed for digital nomads. These events allow individuals to meet like-minded professionals, share experiences, and collaborate on projects. These networking opportunities can lead to new business ventures, freelance gigs, or remote positions.

Cost Savings:

Digital nomads can often benefit from lower living costs by residing in countries with more affordable economies. For example, a digital nomad from New York might decide to live in Medellín, Colombia, where the cost of living is significantly lower. This cost-saving potential allows nomads to enjoy a higher quality of life while spending less on essentials like rent, food, and transportation.

Additionally, some digital nomads adopt minimalistic lifestyles, reducing their expenses by limiting possessions and focusing on experiences rather than material goods.

Economic and Cultural Benefits

The economic benefits of the digital nomad lifestyle extend beyond personal satisfaction. Digital nomads contribute to local economies by spending money on accommodation, food, transportation, and leisure activities. This spending influx can significantly impact small businesses' livelihoods in tourist-heavy regions. For instance, a digital nomad residing in a beach town in Mexico may rent a local apartment, dine at neighborhood restaurants, and use local services, thus injecting cash into the local economy.

Supporting Local Economies

Job Creation and Boosted Income:
Digital nomads often support local employment by hiring locals for various services, such as transportation, housekeeping, cooking, and language lessons. This creates job opportunities and provides a steady income stream for residents in popular digital nomad destinations like Bali, Chiang Mai, and Lisbon.
Co-working spaces catering to digital nomads also contribute to the local economy by renting commercial properties, employing staff, and hosting events that attract locals and travelers.

Increased Demand for Services:
The presence of digital nomads often drives demand for modern services such as high-speed internet, international banking, and health and wellness facilities. This demand encourages local governments and businesses to invest in infrastructure improvements, benefiting nomads and residents.
Some cities, like Medellín and Prague, have actively improved internet infrastructure, created digital nomad hubs, and offered incentives to attract remote workers, recognizing the economic benefits they bring.

Fostering Cultural Exchange

Sharing Knowledge and Skills:
Digital nomads often share their skills and knowledge with locals through formal workshops, casual conversations, or collaborative projects. This exchange of ideas can lead to innovative solutions for local challenges, ranging from entrepreneurship initiatives to educational programs.

In addition to sharing professional skills, digital nomads often act as informal ambassadors of their home cultures, introducing local communities to different traditions, foods, and customs.

Increased Global Awareness:
Engaging with different communities enhances empathy and creativity, often resulting in innovative ideas that benefit both the nomads and the residents. Digital nomads become cultural bridges, fostering mutual understanding and tolerance.

For example, a digital nomad in environmental consulting might collaborate with local NGOs to address sustainability issues, blending global insights with local knowledge to create effective solutions.

Real-World Example: Amanda's Journey
Consider the case of Amanda, a graphic designer who decided to embrace the digital nomad lifestyle. After transitioning to remote work, she spent six months traveling through Southeast Asia while continuing to serve her clients. Amanda could maintain her professional commitments while exploring new destinations by utilizing tools like Slack for communication, Trello for project management, and Zoom for client meetings. This experience enriched her personal life and enhanced her creativity, allowing her to bring fresh perspectives to her design work.

Immersing in Local Cultures: During her time in Bali, Amanda immersed herself in the local art scene, drawing inspiration from traditional Balinese art forms. By collaborating with local artists, she produced a series of designs that blended her unique style with the vibrant aesthetics of the region. This collaboration boosted her portfolio and allowed her to contribute to the local art community, providing financial support to her partners and generating visibility for their work.

Navigating Challenges: Amanda faced challenges during her journey, such as unstable internet connectivity in remote areas and time zone differences with clients. To overcome these issues, she planned her work schedule around reliable internet locations and adapted her communication to accommodate different time zones. Her experience highlights the adaptability and problem-solving skills required to succeed as a digital nomad.

Challenges of the Digital Nomad Lifestyle

While digital nomadism offers many benefits, it presents several challenges individuals must navigate to maintain a sustainable and fulfilling lifestyle.

Maintaining Routine and Consistency:

Many digital nomads must help maintain a consistent routine while adapting to different time zones and cultural environments. This lack of stability can lead to isolation, particularly for those who find it difficult to build lasting relationships while frequently on the move.

Managing work-life balance becomes increasingly complex when your home and workplace are often the same. For instance, some digital nomads report difficulty separating work time from personal time, which can lead to burnout. Setting boundaries is essential, but this can be challenging in a flexible environment where the line between work and leisure is blurred.

Navigating Practical Challenges:

Digital nomads must also navigate practical considerations such as securing reliable internet access and managing time zones for client meetings. For example, Amanda faced difficulties traveling in remote areas with unstable internet connectivity. To mitigate these issues, she learned to plan her work schedule around reliable internet locations, prioritizing her tasks to accommodate travel days.

Health and safety concerns can also arise, especially for those traveling to regions with different healthcare standards. Digital nomads need health insurance that covers them internationally and consider obtaining vaccinations and preventative medications based on their destination.

Managing Finances and Legalities:

Financial management can be complicated for digital nomads, as they may need to deal with multiple currencies, banking systems, and tax regulations. To avoid legal issues, it is essential to clearly understand income tax obligations in both home and host countries.

Some countries have implemented special digital nomad visas that make it easier for remote workers to live and work legally while contributing to the local economy. Understanding visa requirements and maintaining proper documentation is crucial for a smooth digital nomad experience.

The Future of Digital Nomadism

Looking ahead, the trend of digital nomadism is expected to grow as more people prioritize flexibility and work-life balance. Governments and local communities are beginning to recognize the potential economic benefits of attracting digital nomads, leading to initiatives that offer special visas and support services for remote workers. Countries like Estonia, Barbados, and Georgia have launched digital nomad visa programs, allowing individuals to live and work legally while contributing to local economies.

Increased Support for Digital Nomads:

Numerous companies have developed resources to support digital nomads in response to this growing movement. Platforms like Nomad List, Remote OK, and SafetyWing provide insights into the best cities for remote work, considering factors like cost of living, internet quality, and community presence.

Co-living spaces specifically designed for digital nomads are also on the rise. These spaces offer accommodation, co-working facilities, and community events. These spaces provide a sense of community and support, helping nomads connect with others who share similar lifestyles and challenges.

Sustainable Digital Nomadism:

As the digital nomad movement grows, there is a growing emphasis on sustainable travel and responsible tourism. Digital nomads are encouraged to minimize their environmental impact by reducing air travel, supporting eco-friendly accommodations, and engaging in local conservation efforts.

Additionally, digital nomads can contribute positively to local communities by volunteering, supporting local businesses, and respecting cultural norms. This approach promotes ethical digital nomadism, ensuring that the lifestyle benefits both the nomads and the regions they inhabit.

Digital nomadism represents a revolutionary shift in how we perceive work and lifestyle. While it offers incredible exploration and personal development opportunities, it also requires careful planning and adaptability. By leveraging technology, building a supportive community, and proactively addressing challenges, digital nomads can thrive in this new work paradigm. As more professionals embrace this lifestyle, the future of work will continue to evolve, transforming individual lives and the fabric of our global economy. The rise of digital nomadism is not just a trend; it reflects a more profound societal change toward valuing flexibility, connection, and the pursuit of meaningful experiences in both work and life.

Challenges Faced by Digital Nomads

Despite the many benefits, digital nomadism also presents challenges. Maintaining a work-life balance can be difficult, as the boundaries between work and leisure become blurred.

Additionally, digital nomads must navigate visa restrictions, internet connectivity, and the potential for isolation. To thrive in this lifestyle, individuals must develop strong time management skills and self-discipline, ensuring they can meet professional obligations while enjoying the freedom of travel.

Digital nomads often face unique challenges, such as navigating visa regulations that can limit their ability to work in certain countries. For instance, many countries have strict rules regarding work permits, and failure to comply can result in fines or deportation. This necessitates a careful balance between enjoying the local culture and meeting work obligations.

The Future of Remote Work

As we look to the future, several key trends are emerging that will shape the remote work landscape. Understanding these trends is crucial for employees and organizations aiming to remain competitive and relevant in an ever-evolving work environment. This analysis delves deeper into three primary areas: AI integration, virtual reality (VR) collaboration tools, and evolving co-working models.

AI Integration

Artificial Intelligence (AI) is set to revolutionize remote work by automating routine tasks, enhancing productivity, and improving decision-making processes. As AI tools become more sophisticated, they enable employees to focus on higher-level strategic tasks, freeing time for creativity and innovation. Implementing AI in the workplace can lead to streamlined workflows, more informed decision-making, and reduced operational costs.

Critical Applications of AI in Remote Work

Task Automation:
AI increasingly automates repetitive tasks like data entry, scheduling, managing emails, and processing documents. This

automation saves significant time and reduces human error, allowing employees to concentrate on more complex and strategic tasks.

AI-powered personal assistants, such as Microsoft's Cortana and Google Assistant, and AI scheduling tools like Clara can help manage calendars, set reminders, schedule meetings, and suggest optimal meeting times based on participant availability. For example, AI assistants can reschedule appointments based on changing priorities without requiring manual input.

In customer service roles, AI chatbots, like those developed by Zendesk and Intercom, can manage basic inquiries, troubleshoot issues, and provide real-time support to customers. This significantly improves response times, allowing human agents to handle more complex problems.

Performance Analytics:
AI tools can analyze team performance data to identify bottlenecks and suggest improvements. For instance, platforms like Monday.com and ClickUp use AI algorithms to analyze task completion rates, team dynamics, and workflow efficiency. Managers can use these insights to refine processes, reassign tasks, or offer targeted training, ultimately enhancing productivity and team morale.

AI-driven analytics can also predict potential delays or performance issues based on historical data, enabling proactive adjustments. This predictive capability helps teams stay on track, meet deadlines, and manage workloads effectively, especially in project management scenarios.

AI can also be used for sentiment analysis, employee feedback, and team morale. For example, AI tools like Officevibe and TINYpulse analyze employee survey results to identify job satisfaction, engagement, and potential burnout trends, helping managers address issues before they escalate.

Personalization:
AI can tailor the work experience to individual employees by analyzing user behavior, preferences, and performance metrics. For instance, AI tools can recommend personalized learning materials, suggest relevant resources, or even collaborate with team members with complementary skills.

Regarding career development, AI-powered platforms like LinkedIn Learning use machine learning algorithms to suggest courses that align with an employee's role, skills, and career aspirations. This personalized approach enhances employee engagement and drives skill development and retention.

AI can also assist in designing personalized workflows by adapting to individual work habits. For example, AI tools like Motion learn from a user's daily activities and create customized schedules that optimize productivity, such as efficiently allocating focus time for deep work or clustering meetings.

Real-World Example: AI Integration in Remote Work
A prime example of AI integration in remote work is using chatbots for customer support. Companies like Zendesk and Intercom have developed AI-powered chatbots that handle routine inquiries, allowing human agents to focus on more complex issues. This not only improves response times but also enhances customer satisfaction. For instance:

- AI chatbots can answer frequently asked questions instantly, provide information about services, and guide customers through troubleshooting processes. This ensures customers receive 24/7 support, even when human agents are unavailable.
- AI can analyze customer interactions to identify common pain points and suggest improvements to service delivery. This feedback loop enables companies to continuously refine their customer support strategies, resulting in better user experiences.

AI integration extends beyond customer service. In

recruitment, AI tools like HireVue use natural language processing to assess candidate responses in interviews, evaluating what is said and how it is said. This helps hiring teams make more informed decisions, even in remote hiring processes.

Virtual Reality (VR) Collaboration Tools

Virtual Reality is set to transform how remote teams collaborate, offering immersive virtual environments that mimic in-person interactions. VR tools make remote collaboration more engaging, effective, and dynamic, enabling everything from meetings and brainstorming sessions to training and team-building activities.

Expanding VR Applications in Remote Work

Immersive Meetings:
Traditional video calls often need more engagement in face-to-face interactions. VR meetings, however, offer a fully immersive experience where participants feel like they are in the same room. This sense of presence fosters stronger connections, makes meetings more engaging, and enhances communication by capturing non-verbal cues like gestures and body language.

For example, platforms like **Spatial**, **Horizon Workrooms** by Meta, and **Glue** offer virtual meeting rooms where participants can interact using avatars. These VR environments allow users to use virtual whiteboards, share screens, and manipulate 3D objects collaboratively.

Beyond traditional meetings, VR is being used for virtual conferences and large-scale events. Attendees can move between virtual booths, attend keynote speeches, and network with others in realistic 3D spaces. This immersive experience brings back spontaneity and social interactions often lost in digital conferences.

Enhanced Creativity and Brainstorming:
VR enables teams to visualize concepts in 3D and interact

with digital prototypes. This ability to manipulate objects and experiment in real time is a game-changer for design, architecture, and engineering teams, leading to more creative solutions and faster iterations.

Teams can create and interact with 3D models, virtual prototypes, and interactive simulations in real-time. For example, architects can use VR to walk through building designs, allowing clients to experience the project before it is built.

VR tools like **Miro VR** and **Engage** offer collaborative spaces where participants can draw, move objects, and brainstorm ideas in a shared virtual environment. This boosts creativity and makes the brainstorming process more dynamic and inclusive.

Training and Development:
 VR is also being used for employee training and onboarding. Virtual training modules can simulate real-world scenarios like customer interactions, technical operations, or emergency procedures. This immersive learning experience helps employees gain practical skills in a risk-free environment.

 Industries like healthcare, manufacturing, and aviation already use VR to train employees on complex machinery, surgical procedures, or flight simulations. By practicing in a realistic yet controlled setting, employees develop confidence and competence that translate to better performance in real situations.

Team Building and Social Interaction:
 VR tools can facilitate fun and interactive team-building exercises. Companies can create virtual escape rooms, collaborative games, or team challenges that encourage cooperation and camaraderie.

 Virtual co-working spaces in VR allow remote teams to experience a shared virtual office. These digital workspaces foster a sense of presence and belonging, helping teams bond and maintain a cohesive culture despite geographical distances.

Companies like **Spatial** and **Gather** have developed platforms that offer virtual spaces for remote teams to collaborate in a 3D environment. In **Spatial**, teams can meet in customizable rooms replicating physical meeting spaces, complete with virtual whiteboards, interactive models, and file-sharing capabilities. This immersive environment enables teams to brainstorm, design, and strategize as if they were physically together.

In a more playful application, **Rec Room**, a VR social platform, offers companies the ability to conduct team-building exercises in virtual worlds, such as participating in mini-games or virtual scavenger hunts. These activities boost team morale and improve communication and trust among team members.

Evolving Co-Working Models

The rise of remote work has led to the evolution of co-working spaces, which now cater to hybrid workers and digital nomads seeking flexibility, community, and professional development. These modern co-working spaces offer a middle ground between traditional office settings and working from home, providing professionals with flexible memberships, networking opportunities, and wellness programs.

Characteristics of Next-Gen Co-Working Spaces

Flexible Membership Models:
Co-working spaces now offer a range of flexible membership options, such as hot desks, dedicated desks, private offices, and meeting rooms that can be booked on demand. These spaces accommodate various work styles, from solo freelancers to entire remote teams.

Some co-working spaces provide "pay-as-you-go" models, allowing individuals to use the facilities as needed without long-term commitments. This flexibility caters to professionals who require occasional office space, such as during client meetings or collaborative sessions.

Community Building and Networking Events:
Modern co-working spaces prioritize community engagement by hosting networking events, workshops, panel discussions, and social gatherings. These events foster collaboration, knowledge sharing, and personal development among members.

Spaces like **Impact Hub** and **WeWork** have built strong communities where members can find potential collaborators, mentors, or clients. They host regular events like "Pitch Nights," where entrepreneurs can present ideas to investors, or "Skill Shares," where members teach workshops on their areas of expertise.

Wellness Initiatives and Amenities:
Recognizing the importance of mental and physical well-being, many co-working spaces offer wellness programs such as yoga classes, meditation sessions, fitness facilities, and on-site childcare. These initiatives aim to create a more balanced work environment and promote productivity and well-being.

For example, **Second Home** co-working spaces offer green workspaces filled with natural light and plant life, creating a serene environment that supports mental wellness. Some spaces even have outdoor working areas, allowing members to work in nature.

Hybrid and Remote Support Services:
Co-working spaces have adapted to support hybrid work models by offering virtual memberships, where remote members can access online events, digital networking opportunities, and virtual co-working sessions.

Spaces like **Regus** provide virtual office services, including mail handling, reception support, and access to meeting rooms worldwide, supporting businesses that operate remotely while maintaining a physical presence.

Spaces like **WeWork**, **Impact Hub**, and **Industrious** have redefined co-working by offering flexible memberships, robust community events, and wellness programs that cater to remote and hybrid workers.

WeWork has partnered with various wellness brands to offer on-site fitness classes, mental health resources, and guided meditation sessions. This approach supports productivity and promotes a healthier work-life balance.

Impact Hub, focused on social entrepreneurship, has created a global network of co-working spaces that provide office facilities, mentorship, funding opportunities, and collaborative projects for startups aiming to create social impact.

Emerging technologies and evolving workplace models will shape the future of remote work. AI integration, VR collaboration tools, and flexible co-working spaces are just some trends that will redefine how and where we work. By embracing these innovations, employees and organizations can enhance productivity, foster creativity, and build a more adaptable and resilient work culture. As remote work evolves, staying informed about these trends will be crucial for maintaining competitiveness and achieving long-term success.

Virtual Reality (VR) Collaboration Tools

Virtual reality is poised to transform how remote teams collaborate, offering a more immersive and interactive alternative to traditional communication methods. With VR tools, employees can engage in virtual environments that replicate real-world interactions, helping bridge the gap often felt in remote work settings. This technology is useful for meetings, brainstorming sessions, project management, training, and team-building activities.

The Impact of VR on Remote Collaboration

VR technology allows for the creation of virtual spaces that simulate in-person environments. These digital spaces give users a sense of "presence," making remote collaboration more engaging and effective. Unlike video calls, which can feel impersonal and lack non-verbal cues, VR meetings allow participants to read body language and interact in ways that mirror real-life conversations. By using avatars that can move, gesture, and even make eye contact, users can experience more dynamic and meaningful interactions.

Advantages of VR Collaboration Tools

Immersive Meetings:
Traditional video calls often need to capture the energy and engagement of face-to-face interactions. VR meetings provide an immersive experience where participants feel in the same room, fostering a sense of presence and connection. This can be particularly beneficial for remote teams that require frequent collaboration, such as project management or creative brainstorming sessions.

In a VR meeting, users can stand around a virtual whiteboard and use virtual markers to draw, write, and move objects in 3D space to illustrate concepts more effectively. This can create a more interactive and engaging meeting atmosphere, reducing fatigue and promoting active participation.

Enhanced Creativity:
Virtual environments can stimulate creativity by allowing team members to visualize concepts in 3D and interact with digital prototypes. This feature is precious for design, architecture, and engineering teams, who can manipulate models, conduct virtual walkthroughs, or simulate various scenarios.

For product development teams, VR tools can facilitate the

design process by enabling participants to view prototypes from multiple angles, make real-time adjustments, and collaborate more effectively. This type of hands-on interaction fosters creativity and innovation, as team members can experiment with ideas in a virtual setting before moving to physical prototypes.

Training and Onboarding:
VR can enhance training and onboarding processes by simulating real-life scenarios like customer interactions, safety procedures, or technical operations. Employees can learn in a controlled environment that mirrors their work conditions, leading to more effective training outcomes.

For example, VR training modules can simulate emergencies or complex machinery operations, allowing employees to practice their responses in a safe and immersive space. This can be particularly useful for industries like healthcare, manufacturing, and customer service, where practical training is essential.

Team Building:
VR tools can facilitate team-building exercises in a fun and interactive way. Companies can create virtual escape rooms, collaborative games, or team challenges that encourage cooperation, problem-solving, and camaraderie. These activities can help break the monotony of remote work and strengthen team bonds, leading to better collaboration and communication. Virtual team-building events, such as scavenger hunts or trivia games, can also include customized themes and scenarios that align with the company's culture and values, further enhancing engagement and morale.

Real-World Example: VR Platforms in Action

Consider companies like **Spatial**, **Gather**, and **Horizon Workrooms**, which offer virtual collaboration spaces where teams can meet and work together in a 3D environment.

These platforms provide a range of features, from interactive whiteboards and 3D models to virtual breakout rooms and networking areas.

Spatial allows users to create realistic virtual spaces where teams can interact as if they were in the same physical room. Using customizable avatars, which can mimic facial expressions and body movements, enables individuals to express themselves more thoroughly than in a traditional video call.

Gather provides customizable virtual rooms where teams can brainstorm, socialize, or conduct meetings. With features like spatial audio (where sounds come from specific directions, simulating real-life interactions) and collaborative tools, Gather makes remote interactions more dynamic and engaging.

Horizon Workrooms, developed by Meta, offers a VR meeting room experience that allows participants to use virtual whiteboards, share screens, and even bring physical keyboards into the VR space for seamless transitions between virtual and physical work.

Using avatars in these virtual spaces enhances communication and encourages creativity and engagement. Avatars provide a sense of identity and presence in the virtual world, making it easier for participants to build rapport and collaborate effectively.

Evolving Co-Working Models

The rise of remote work has led to the evolution of co-working spaces, which now cater to the needs of hybrid workers seeking flexibility, community, and professional development. These modern co-working spaces offer a middle ground between traditional office settings and working from home, providing professionals with flexible membership options, networking opportunities, and wellness initiatives.

Characteristics of Modern Co-Working Spaces

Flexibility:
Modern co-working spaces offer flexible membership options, allowing individuals and companies to rent office space daily, weekly, or monthly. This flexibility is precious for startups, freelancers, and remote teams that may need to scale their office space based on demand.

Many co-working spaces now offer "hot desks," dedicated desks, private offices, and meeting rooms that can be booked on demand. This model accommodates various work styles and schedules, supporting solo workers and larger teams.

Community Engagement:
A key characteristic of co-working spaces is their focus on building community among members. These spaces often host networking events, workshops, panel discussions, and social gatherings to encourage collaboration and knowledge sharing among diverse professionals.

Co-working spaces can act as hubs for innovation, bringing together individuals from different industries who can share insights, form partnerships, and collaborate on projects. This sense of community particularly appeals to remote workers who miss the social aspect of traditional office environments.

Wellness Initiatives:
Recognizing the importance of mental health, many co-working spaces have begun incorporating wellness programs such as yoga classes, meditation rooms, fitness facilities, and relaxation zones. These initiatives aim to create a more balanced work environment, promoting productivity and well-being.

Some spaces even offer on-site childcare, therapy sessions, and nutritional workshops, making it easier for professionals to maintain a healthy work-life balance.

Support Services for Startups and Freelancers:
Modern co-working spaces often provide additional services like mentorship programs, access to venture capital networks,

and business development workshops. These services can be invaluable for startups and freelancers looking to grow their businesses and expand their professional networks.

Some co-working spaces also offer accelerator programs, which provide funding, guidance, and resources to early-stage startups. This model supports individual entrepreneurs and fosters a culture of innovation and entrepreneurship within the co-working community.

Spaces like **WeWork**, **Regus**, and **Impact Hub** are at the forefront of this trend, providing flexible memberships that allow individuals and teams to use shared office facilities as needed.

WeWork offers various co-working solutions, from hot desks to private offices. The company has also introduced wellness initiatives, partnering with health and wellness companies to provide yoga classes, meditation sessions, and mental health resources. These services support members' physical and psychological well-being, making co-working more than a workplace.

Regus, a global co-working network, offers flexible office spaces in major cities worldwide. The company's focus on community-building is evident through its regular networking events, workshops, and industry-specific meetups, which encourage collaboration among members.

Impact Hub, which caters to social entrepreneurs and startups, emphasizes sustainability and social impact. With a strong focus on community, Impact Hub provides programs, events, and mentorship to support entrepreneurs working on projects with a positive societal impact.

As remote work continues to grow, co-working spaces will likely become an integral part of the work ecosystem, catering to remote employees and companies seeking flexible office solutions. The evolving co-working model addresses the need for physical workspace and fosters personal and professional development by providing access to networking, learning, and wellness opportunities.

The Future of VR and Co-Working

Integrating VR collaboration tools and evolving co-working models represents a shift toward more flexible and immersive work environments. As VR technology becomes more accessible and co-working spaces continue to innovate, the lines between physical and virtual workspaces blur, creating new possibilities for how teams collaborate and connect.

- **Hybrid Co-Working Spaces**: In the future, co-working spaces may incorporate VR rooms where members can engage in virtual meetings, training, or collaborative projects with remote colleagues. This hybrid approach would combine the physical benefits of co-working with the immersive potential of VR, offering a more holistic work experience.
- **Personalized VR Workspaces**: Advances in VR technology could lead to the development of personalized virtual workspaces, where remote workers can customize their surroundings, tools, and interactions. This would allow for a more tailored and efficient work experience, regardless of physical location.

As these trends continue to develop, remote teams will have even more opportunities to enhance collaboration, foster innovation, and build meaningful connections, making the future of work more inclusive, flexible, and engaging.

Adapting for Tomorrow

As we navigate the rapidly changing world of remote work, it becomes increasingly crucial for employees and organizations to cultivate a mindset centered around continuous learning and adaptability. The work environment is no longer static; it is dynamic and requires proactive strategies to ensure relevance and competitiveness. Below are comprehensive strategies to empower individuals and teams to thrive in this evolving landscape.

Embrace Lifelong Learning

The importance of lifelong learning cannot be overstated in today's fast-paced work environment. As technology and work practices evolve, employees must continuously update their skills to remain relevant and practical. Organizations can play a significant role in fostering a learning culture by providing various resources and opportunities for professional development.

Critical Components of Lifelong Learning:

Access to Resources: Companies can partner with e-learning platforms like LinkedIn Learning, Coursera, or Udemy to provide employees with various courses. From technical skills such as programming languages, data analysis, and cybersecurity to essential soft skills like emotional intelligence, negotiation, and leadership, employees can tailor their learning experiences to fit their career goals. This approach encourages a culture of self-improvement, motivating employees to take ownership of their professional development.

In-House Training Programs: Many organizations develop training initiatives tailored to their industry needs. For example, a technology company might implement an internal coding boot camp to elevate employees' programming skills. Such programs enhance individual capabilities and encourage team bonding as colleagues learn and grow together.

Mentorship and Coaching: Establishing mentorship programs within organizations can provide employees with personalized guidance from experienced professionals. These relationships foster knowledge sharing and help employees navigate their career paths effectively. For instance, pairing new hires with seasoned mentors can significantly ease the onboarding process and facilitate cultural integration within the company.

Certification Programs: Encouraging employees to pursue certifications related to their roles can add credibility and enhance their expertise. Many industries have specific certifications, such as Project Management Professional (PMP), Certified Information Systems Security Professional (CISSP), or Six Sigma, that can provide employees with valuable credentials, opening doors to new opportunities.

Companies like Google and Amazon emphasize continuous learning by offering comprehensive training and development programs. Google's "Career Guru" initiative connects employees with mentors across various departments, facilitating cross-functional knowledge sharing. By investing in employees' growth, organizations cultivate a skilled and adaptable workforce ready to meet the challenges of an ever-changing market.

Stay Informed About Industry Trends

In addition to enhancing individual skills, staying informed about industry trends and emerging technologies is essential for employees seeking to maintain a competitive edge. Awareness of the latest developments can provide valuable insights, enabling proactive adaptation and strategic planning.

Strategies for Staying Informed:

Subscribe to Industry Publications: Employees should regularly read industry journals, newsletters, and blogs to stay current on-field trends and advancements. Resources such as the Harvard Business Review, MIT Sloan Management Review, and industry-specific publications offer critical analyses and forecasts that can inform decision-making.

Attend Webinars and Conferences: Participating in virtual and in-person conferences and webinars enables employees to learn from experts and network with peers. These events often feature panels, workshops, and keynote speeches that address pressing issues and innovative practices within the industry.

Join Professional Organizations: Becoming a professional association member provides access to resources, training programs, and networking opportunities. Many associations host regular events, offering members insights into industry standards and best practices while creating collaboration and knowledge-sharing avenues.

Engage on Professional Social Networks: Utilizing platforms like LinkedIn to follow industry leaders, join relevant groups, and engage in discussions can help employees stay informed about trends and expand their professional networks. Sharing insights and articles and participating in discussions can enhance visibility within the industry.

Subscribing to platforms like Harvard Business Review or participating in events like the Remote Work Summit equips employees with the necessary knowledge to navigate the evolving work landscape effectively. Networking at these events can also foster collaborations that further enrich professional development and create opportunities for career advancement.

Cultivate Resilience and Adaptability

Adapting to change is a fundamental skill in today's workforce. Resilience enables employees to cope with challenges and empowers them to thrive in uncertain environments. Organizations can cultivate resilience through various strategies promoting growth and adaptability.

Building a Culture of Resilience:

Encourage a Growth Mindset: Organizations should foster an environment where employees view challenges as opportunities for growth. This mindset can be encouraged through training programs that focus on developing problem-solving skills, emotional intelligence, and creative thinking. By celebrating failures as learning experiences, organizations can promote a culture of innovation.

Foster Psychological Safety: It is crucial to create a workplace where employees feel safe expressing their ideas, taking risks, and discussing challenges without fear of retribution. Psychological safety encourages open communication, collaboration, and the sharing of diverse perspectives, which are essential for resilience.

Implement Regular Feedback Mechanisms: Establishing channels for regular feedback helps employees understand their performance and areas for improvement. Constructive feedback encourages personal and professional growth while reinforcing a culture of continuous improvement.

Encourage Flexibility: Organizations should embrace flexible work arrangements, allowing employees to adapt their schedules to meet personal and professional demands. This flexibility can help reduce stress and enhance overall job satisfaction, enabling employees to manage their responsibilities more effectively.

Promote Well-Being Initiatives: Offering wellness programs that address mental, emotional, and physical health can significantly contribute to employee resilience. Programs may include mindfulness training, stress management workshops, and access to mental health resources.

Companies like Google prioritize resilience by creating cross-functional teams that tackle diverse projects. This structure allows employees to broaden their skill sets and adapt to changing circumstances, ultimately enhancing their ability to thrive in a dynamic work environment. Organizations cultivate a more versatile and agile workforce by providing opportunities for employees to work on various projects.

As remote work continues to evolve, staying ahead of

trends is essential for employees and organizations. Embracing digital nomadism, anticipating changes in remote work, and adapting to new technologies will help individuals navigate the complexities of this new work landscape. By fostering a continuous learning and adaptability culture, organizations can empower their teams to thrive in an increasingly remote and digitally driven future.

References

1. IWG. (2020). *The Future of Work: The Rise of Remote Work and the Digital Nomad*. International Workplace Group.
2. Smith, J. (2021). *The Remote Work Revolution: How to Thrive in a New Normal*. Remote Work Journal.
3. Adams, S. (2021). *Peer Recognition Programs: Boosting Employee Morale in Remote Teams*. Remote Work Journal.
4. Garcia, M. (2021). *Building Trust in Remote Teams: Strategies for Success*. Forbes.
5. Taylor, P. (2020). *Performance Evaluations in Remote Work: Adapting to New Norms*. Journal of Business Psychology.

CHAPTER 9: BALANCING TEAM DYNAMICS IN A HYBRID WORKPLACE

As the modern workplace evolves, hybrid work models are increasingly becoming the norm. This shift presents both exciting opportunities and unique challenges, particularly when it comes to team dynamics. In a hybrid environment, where some team members work remotely while others are in the office, leaders must be adept at navigating the complexities of diverse work styles, preferences, and backgrounds. This chapter will explore practical strategies for managing diverse teams, enhancing team cohesion, and promoting inclusion within hybrid workplaces.

Managing Diverse Teams

In today's rapidly changing work environment, the workforce has become increasingly diverse, encompassing various backgrounds, experiences, and perspectives. This diversity can significantly enrich the workplace, introducing innovative ideas and solutions that foster creativity and drive organizational success. However, managing a diverse team effectively requires a nuanced approach to ensure every team member feels valued and understood, preventing misunderstandings and enhancing collaboration.

Understanding Work Preferences

Different generations within the workforce often exhibit distinct work preferences, communication styles, and attitudes toward collaboration. These generational differences can manifest in various ways, affecting how team members engage with each other and approach their work. For instance:

Baby Boomers: Typically born between 1946 and 1964, this generation often values traditional communication methods and prefers face-to-face meetings for discussions and updates. They have a wealth of experience and may appreciate structured work environments where they can share their knowledge with younger colleagues.

Generation X: Born between 1965 and 1980, Gen Xers are often characterized by adaptability and independence. They value a balance between work and life and may prefer flexible working arrangements that allow them to manage their responsibilities alongside their professional obligations. They also tend to appreciate direct communication and quick responses to their inquiries.

Millennials (Generation Y): Born between 1981 and 1996, Millennials are known for their comfort with technology and digital communication. They often favor collaborative tools like Slack and Zoom for ongoing communication and project management. This generation typically seeks meaningful work and values feedback and recognition for their contributions.

Generation Z: The youngest workforce, born from 1997 onward, tends to be even more tech-savvy than Millennials. They often prefer communication through digital platforms and social media. They will also likely prioritize inclusivity and social responsibility in their work environments.

Recognizing and embracing these generational differences

can enhance team collaboration and productivity (Ng & Burke, 2010). Understanding how team members prefer to communicate and work can help managers design strategies that accommodate these preferences, leading to a more cohesive and productive team.

Consider a project team composed of Baby Boomers, Generation Xers, and Millennials. In this scenario, a Baby Boomer may prefer traditional weekly in-person updates to discuss project progress and address face-to-face challenges. On the other hand, a Millennial team member might advocate for utilizing collaborative platforms like Slack for ongoing communication and quick updates, arguing that this approach would allow for greater flexibility and efficiency.

A manager can facilitate discussions considering each generation's different work preferences to create a harmonious environment and ensure effective collaboration among diverse team members. Here is how the manager could approach this:

Establish Open Communication: The manager can initiate a team meeting to discuss communication preferences openly. This meeting would allow team members to express their preferred methods of communication and share any challenges they face in the current setup. This dialogue can create a sense of inclusivity and encourage team members to feel comfortable voicing their opinions.

Create a Mixed Communication Plan: The manager can design a communication plan incorporating in-person and digital interactions based on the team's input. For example, the team might agree on bi-weekly in-person meetings for in-depth discussions and weekly check-ins via Slack for quick updates and feedback. This balanced approach ensures that all team members feel engaged and included.

Leverage Technology for Collaboration: The manager can introduce collaborative tools catering to different generations' preferences. For instance, utilizing project management software like Trello or Asana can help the team track progress visually and allow team members to comment and provide feedback asynchronously. This versatility accommodates those who prefer traditional methods and those who thrive in a digital environment.

Encourage Mentorship Opportunities: To bridge the generational gap, the manager can implement a mentorship program where Baby Boomers share their expertise with younger team members. This program can enhance knowledge transfer and build relationships across generations, fostering mutual respect and collaboration.

Provide Continuous Training: The manager should consider training sessions addressing different communication styles and generational dynamics. Such training can equip team members with the skills needed to navigate misunderstandings and enhance interpersonal relationships within the team.

Foster a Culture of Feedback: Encouraging regular feedback among team members can help address emerging conflicts or misunderstandings. Creating an environment where constructive criticism is welcomed and appreciated fosters collaboration and strengthens team bonds.

Celebrate Diversity: Recognizing and celebrating each team member's unique contributions is vital. By highlighting individual achievements and promoting an inclusive culture, the manager reinforces the value of diversity and encourages team members to appreciate each other's strengths.

By implementing these strategies, the manager can successfully navigate the complexities of managing a diverse team. The ability to harmonize differing preferences and foster effective communication will enhance productivity and create a workplace culture that values diversity as a critical driver of success.

Addressing Challenges in Diverse Teams

While diversity in the workplace can drive innovation and creativity, it can also present challenges that must be effectively managed. These challenges often stem from differences in communication styles, work ethics, and approaches to conflict resolution. Leaders must cultivate an inclusive environment that acknowledges these differences and actively seeks to leverage them for the benefit of the team and organization. Here are several strategies to address challenges that may arise in diverse teams:

Open Communication and Safe Spaces

One of the foundational aspects of managing a diverse team is fostering an environment of open communication. Team members should feel safe expressing their thoughts, concerns, and feedback without fear of judgment or retaliation. Establishing regular check-ins and feedback sessions can significantly enhance this open dialogue.

Implementing a structured feedback system, such as anonymous surveys, can help team members voice concerns or suggestions they might hesitate to express in person. This feedback loop ensures that leaders are aware of potential issues and can address them proactively.

Creating "safe spaces" for diversity, equity, and inclusion discussions can also be beneficial. These spaces encourage team members to share their experiences and perspectives, fostering a deeper understanding of one another. For instance, leaders can hold monthly diversity dialogues where team members can discuss their backgrounds, cultural influences, and how these affect their work styles and preferences.

Regular Team-Building Exercises

Team-building exercises are essential for improving collaboration among diverse groups. These activities can help break down barriers, build trust, and foster camaraderie. By participating in exercises that require teamwork and communication, employees can learn more about each other's strengths and working styles.

A technology firm might organize offsite retreats focusing on team-building activities. These could include problem-solving challenges, trust-building exercises, or fun activities like escape rooms. Such experiences enhance teamwork and allow employees to bond in a more relaxed setting, making communicating and collaborating easier in the workplace.

Moreover, virtual team-building activities can be just as practical for remote teams. Online games, quizzes, or collaborative projects can foster engagement and connectivity among team members, regardless of their physical location. Incorporating icebreakers and team challenges in regular meetings can help maintain team cohesion.

Diversity Circles

Implementing "diversity circles" is an effective strategy to facilitate dialogue around diversity within teams. These circles bring together team members to discuss their work preferences, cultural backgrounds, and how these factors influence their collaboration. This practice promotes mutual understanding and respect among team members.

A technology firm might establish diversity circles that meet bi-weekly to share experiences related to their work and discuss ways to enhance collaboration. Each circle could focus on different themes, such as communication styles, conflict resolution strategies, or cultural competencies. For instance, during one session, team members could share their preferred methods of receiving feedback or handling disagreements. By understanding these preferences, team members can adapt their interactions to accommodate one another better, reducing friction and enhancing teamwork.

Moreover, these circles can serve as platforms for mentorship, where more experienced employees guide newcomers or those from different backgrounds, helping them navigate the organizational culture. This mentorship fosters inclusion and allows for sharing best practices in overcoming common challenges related to diversity.

Conflict Resolution Strategies

Diverse teams may approach conflict differently based on their backgrounds and experiences. Leaders should equip their teams with conflict resolution strategies that embrace diversity rather than shy away from it. Training sessions focusing on cultural competency and conflict resolution can prepare employees to handle disputes more effectively.

Conducting workshops that address different cultural perspectives on conflict resolution can be instrumental. For instance, employees from collectivist cultures may prioritize harmony and group consensus, while those from individualistic cultures might advocate for confrontation and open dialogue. By understanding these differences, team members can adapt their approaches to conflict, ensuring that all voices are heard and respected.

Regular Reflection and Adaptation

Finally, it is crucial for leaders to continuously reflect on the effectiveness of their strategies and be willing to adapt as necessary. Regularly assessing the team's dynamics and gathering feedback on the inclusiveness of the work environment can provide valuable insights into areas that may need improvement.

A company might implement quarterly diversity audits to evaluate the effectiveness of its diversity initiatives. These audits could include employee surveys, focus groups, and performance metrics related to team collaboration and conflict resolution. By analyzing the data collected, leaders can identify trends and make informed decisions about enhancing diversity initiatives.

In conclusion, effectively managing diverse teams requires intentionality and ongoing effort. Organizations can address the challenges associated with diversity by fostering open communication, implementing team-building exercises, creating diversity circles, and providing conflict resolution training. By embracing these strategies, leaders can build a more cohesive, innovative, and productive team that leverages each member's unique strengths.

Enhancing Team Cohesion in Hybrid Environments

Creating a cohesive team is vital for achieving shared goals, particularly in a hybrid environment where employees may not interact face-to-face daily. Team cohesion fosters trust, collaboration, and a sense of belonging, all of which are crucial for the success of any organization. Organizations can employ various strategies to strengthen team cohesion, reinforcing a sense of community and collective purpose.

Building a Shared Mission

A compelling shared mission significantly enhances team cohesion. When employees understand how their contributions align with the organization's objectives, they are more likely to feel invested in their work and committed to the team dynamic. A shared mission provides direction and inspires employees to strive for excellence, fostering a culture of accountability and collaboration.

Organizations like Zappos have built their culture around a clear mission of delivering exceptional customer service. By regularly communicating this mission and recognizing individual contributions, Zappos fosters a sense of community and commitment among employees, regardless of their work location. The company conducts regular "all-hands" meetings to celebrate individual and team successes related to their mission, thus reinforcing the importance of each employee's role in the broader organizational goals.

Moreover, leaders can help instill this sense of shared purpose by engaging employees in the mission-setting process. For instance, a healthcare organization might involve frontline staff in developing their patient care mission, ensuring that the resulting objectives resonate with those who deliver care. This involvement enhances commitment and encourages team members to hold each other accountable for achieving their shared goals.

Utilizing Technology for Connection

Technology is crucial for maintaining connections among team members in a hybrid workplace. The lack of in-person interactions can lead to feelings of isolation, making it essential to leverage technology to foster engagement and collaboration. By implementing various digital tools and platforms, organizations can create opportunities for meaningful interactions that reinforce team cohesion.

Virtual Team-Building Activities:

Regular virtual team-building activities can enhance relationships among team members. These activities range from icebreaker games to more structured challenges to facilitate interaction and collaboration. Platforms like Zoom and Microsoft Teams can host virtual escape rooms, trivia competitions, or team challenges requiring problem-solving and teamwork.

A marketing team at a software company organized a virtual "hackathon" where team members collaborated in small groups to develop innovative marketing strategies. This event allowed employees to collaborate creatively and fostered relationships across different departments. As a result, team members reported feeling more connected and engaged in their roles.

Online Brainstorming Sessions:

Collaborative tools such as Miro or MURAL for online brainstorming sessions can also help strengthen team bonds. These platforms allow team members to contribute ideas visually and interactively, making the process more engaging and inclusive. Leaders can schedule regular brainstorming sessions to gather project input, fostering a sense of ownership among team members.

Consistent Check-Ins:

Regular check-ins are essential for maintaining communication in a hybrid setting. Managers should schedule one-on-one and team meetings to discuss progress, address concerns, and celebrate achievements. These touchpoints ensure that everyone remains aligned with team objectives and helps build rapport among team members.

Social Platforms:

Platforms like Gather and Donut allow virtual social interactions among remote teams, providing casual conversations and bonding opportunities. These tools can create virtual spaces where employees can unwind and connect personally, which must often be added in formal work settings. For instance, a company might establish a "virtual coffee break" schedule where team members can join a casual video call to chat and catch up, mimicking the spontaneous interactions in traditional office environments.

Recognition Programs:

Implementing recognition programs can further enhance team cohesion by celebrating individual and team contributions. Regularly acknowledging achievements—whether through shout-outs in meetings, recognition emails, or award systems—helps foster a culture of appreciation.

A global consulting firm might implement a monthly recognition program in which team members nominate peers who exemplify the company's values. The winners receive public acknowledgment during team meetings, reinforcing behaviors contributing to a positive team culture.

The Role of Leadership in Fostering Cohesion

Leaders play a crucial role in enhancing team cohesion. By modeling inclusive behaviors and actively promoting collaboration, they set the tone for the team environment. Leaders should prioritize open communication, encourage feedback, and empathize with team members' challenges in a hybrid setting. Being approachable and supportive, leaders can help cultivate a sense of belonging and trust among team members.

A manager at a tech startup might hold regular "open office hours" where team members can drop in to discuss concerns or share ideas. This accessibility strengthens relationships and encourages a collaborative culture where everyone feels valued and heard.

Enhancing team cohesion in a hybrid work environment requires intentional strategies that promote connection, collaboration, and a shared sense of purpose. Organizations can create a cohesive team culture that drives success by building a compelling shared mission, utilizing technology for connection, and fostering open communication. With the right approach, hybrid teams can thrive, leveraging their diverse backgrounds and experiences to achieve common goals.

Promoting Inclusion

Inclusion is critical to creating a supportive work environment where all employees feel valued and engaged. In a hybrid workplace, leaders must ensure remote employees do not feel excluded from team dynamics.

Ensuring Equal Participation

One of the main challenges in hybrid teams is ensuring that all members have an equal opportunity to contribute. Remote team members can sometimes feel overlooked during in-person meetings. To address this, leaders should implement strategies that encourage equal participation.

Utilizing video conferencing tools like Zoom can facilitate remote employees' real-time participation. Establishing ground rules encouraging everyone to contribute can foster a more inclusive atmosphere. Leaders might invite remote members to share their thoughts first, ensuring they can speak before in-person colleagues dominate the conversation.

Recognizing and Celebrating Contributions

Acknowledging the achievements of all team members is a vital component of promoting inclusion. Public recognition should be meaningful and highlight the diverse contributions made by employees.

Implementing a recognition program that showcases employee accomplishments—regardless of their physical location—can help create an inclusive atmosphere. This might involve shout-outs during team meetings or highlighting achievements in company newsletters, reinforcing that every contribution is valued.

Effectively balancing team dynamics in a hybrid workplace requires thoughtful strategies and intentional leadership. By managing diverse teams, enhancing cohesion, and promoting inclusion, leaders can create an environment where every employee feels valued and empowered to contribute. As the workplace evolves, adopting these principles will be essential for achieving organizational success and fostering a positive, productive culture.

References

- Ng, E. S., & Burke, R. J. (2010). *Cultural values and work outcomes: A comparison of two generations of Canadian managers. Journal of Managerial Psychology*, 25(5), 548–564.

CHAPTER 10: ENHANCING REMOTE PRODUCTIVITY THROUGH MINDFULNESS

In today's fast-paced and ever-evolving remote work environment, pursuing productivity often comes at the expense of mental well-being. With the rise of telecommuting and hybrid work arrangements, employees face unique challenges that can lead to stress, burnout, and decreased job satisfaction. However, incorporating mindfulness into daily work routines presents a powerful solution to enhance focus, reduce stress, and foster creativity. This chapter will explore the significance of mindfulness at work, practical techniques for integrating mindful practices into everyday life, and the critical role of conscious communication in promoting a harmonious remote work environment.

Mindfulness at Work

Mindfulness is maintaining a moment-by-moment awareness of our thoughts, feelings, bodily sensations, and surrounding environment. In the workplace, mindfulness encourages individuals to be fully present in their tasks, which can lead to improved concentration and productivity. Research indicates that practicing mindfulness can help mitigate stress and improve overall well-being, making it particularly relevant for remote workers who may experience feelings of isolation or disconnection (Kabat-Zinn, 1990).

Improving Focus

In remote work, distractions are omnipresent—whether it is the temptation of household chores, the allure of social media, or the background noise of family members. Mindfulness equips individuals with the tools to tune out these distractions and focus on the task. Studies have shown that mindfulness training can enhance cognitive flexibility, allowing employees to adapt more readily to shifting priorities and challenges (Zeidan et al., 2010).

Consider an employee named Sarah, a software developer who transitioned to remote work during the pandemic. Initially, Sarah struggled with maintaining focus amidst the distractions of her home environment. After committing to a daily mindfulness meditation practice, Sarah reported a marked improvement in her ability to concentrate on complex coding tasks. By dedicating just ten minutes each morning to mindfulness, she could clear her mind of clutter, resulting in increased productivity and a higher quality of work.

Reducing Stress

The transition to remote work has heightened stress levels for many individuals. Mindfulness is an effective stress management tool that promotes relaxation and emotional regulation. Meditation, deep breathing, and mindful movement have been shown to lower cortisol levels, the hormone associated with stress, contributing to a greater sense of calm and well-being (Turakitwanakan et al., 2013).

John, a remote marketing manager, often felt overwhelmed by the pressures of meeting tight deadlines. After attending a workshop on mindfulness, he began incorporating short mindfulness exercises into his workday, such as five-minute breathing breaks between tasks. This practice allowed John to manage his stress levels effectively, leading to improved decision-making and a more positive outlook on his work. His experience underscores the importance of integrating mindfulness as a coping strategy in high-pressure work environments.

Enhancing Creativity

Mindfulness benefits focus and stress reduction and is crucial in fostering creativity. By quieting the mind and reducing mental clutter, individuals can access more profound levels of creativity and innovation. Mindfulness encourages divergent thinking, allowing employees to explore new ideas and solutions without the constraints of self-doubt or fear of failure (Goleman, 2013).

A graphic designer working remotely, Emily often needed help with creative blocks that hindered her ability to produce fresh ideas. After attending mindfulness training sessions, she began implementing mindfulness techniques, including visualization and mindful sketching, into her design process. As a result, Emily discovered a surge in her creative output, enabling her to develop innovative design concepts that exceeded client expectations. This transformation highlights mindfulness's profound impact on enhancing creative problem-solving in remote work settings.

Integrating Mindful Practices

Incorporating mindfulness into the daily routine of remote work can be simple and accessible. Here are some practical techniques to consider:

Meditation

Meditation is a cornerstone of mindfulness, allowing

individuals to cultivate awareness and focus. Even a brief meditation session can significantly impact concentration and stress management. Employees can utilize guided meditation apps like Headspace or Calm to facilitate their practice and establish a consistent routine.

Employees might start their day in a remote setting with a 10-minute guided meditation focused on gratitude and intention-setting. They can approach their tasks with a clear and positive mindset by taking this time to center themselves.

Deep Breathing Exercises
Deep breathing exercises provide an immediate way to alleviate stress and ground oneself during a busy workday. Techniques such as the 4-7-8 method, where one inhales for four counts, holds for seven counts, and exhales for eight counts, can quickly calm the mind and body.

Employees can take a short break during a hectic workday to practice deep breathing. This brief pause reduces stress and enhances clarity, enabling them to tackle tasks more effectively.

Digital Detoxes
In our increasingly digital world, taking intentional breaks from screens is essential for maintaining mental health. A digital detox involves unplugging from all devices for a set period, allowing individuals to recharge and refocus.

Many remote workers might benefit from setting specific times during the day to step away from their screens—whether taking a walk outside or engaging in a non-digital hobby. This practice helps prevent burnout and promotes a healthier work-life balance.

Mindful Communication

Effective communication is vital in any work setting, but it becomes even more crucial in a hybrid environment where misunderstandings can quickly occur. Mindful communication emphasizes clarity, empathy, and active listening, all of which contribute to a more positive and productive work atmosphere.

Practicing Active Listening

Active listening involves fully engaging with the speaker, demonstrating genuine interest, and responding thoughtfully. By practicing active listening, team members can ensure that everyone feels heard and valued, fostering stronger relationships.

In a virtual team meeting, a manager can practice active listening by summarizing each team member's comments and asking follow-up questions. This shows respect for their contributions and enhances team collaboration by ensuring everyone is on the same page.

Communicating with Clarity

Clear and concise communication is essential in a remote environment where messages can easily be misinterpreted. By being mindful of language and tone, team members can reduce the likelihood of misunderstandings and build stronger connections.

Employees should be straightforward and explicit about their intentions when sending emails or messages. For instance, instead of saying, "We need to discuss this later," a more effective message would be, "Let us schedule a meeting on Thursday at 3 PM to discuss this in detail." This level of clarity helps set clear expectations and avoids potential confusion.

Encouraging Open Dialogue

Creating a culture of open dialogue encourages team members to express their thoughts and concerns without fear of judgment. Leaders should promote an environment where feedback is welcomed, and diverse perspectives are celebrated.

During team check-ins, a leader can invite team members to share their thoughts on recent projects or suggest improvements. Leaders can foster a sense of inclusion and respect within the team by actively soliciting input and acknowledging contributions.

Integrating mindfulness into remote work is a personal benefit and a strategic advantage for organizations. By cultivating a culture of mindfulness, employees can enhance their focus, reduce stress, and improve communication, ultimately leading to a more productive and harmonious work environment. As remote work continues to be a significant aspect of our professional lives, embracing mindfulness can empower individuals and teams to thrive in this new landscape.

References

- Goleman, D. (2013). *Focus: The Hidden Driver of Excellence*. HarperCollins.
- Turakitwanakan, W., Chantanachai, P., & Harnmongkol, P. (2013). Effect of mindfulness meditation on cortisol levels in healthy individuals: A systematic review. *The Journal of Alternative and Complementary Medicine*, 19(2), 103-111.
- Zeidan, F., Johnson, S. K., Diamond, B. J., David, S. W., & Goolkasian, P. (2010). Mindfulness meditation improves cognition: Evidence of brief mental training. *Consciousness and Cognition*, 19(2), 597-605.

CHAPTER 11: FINANCIAL PLANNING FOR REMOTE WORKERS

As the shift towards remote work reshapes the professional landscape, it presents unique financial challenges and opportunities. Unlike traditional office-based jobs, remote work impacts various aspects of personal finance, such as budgeting, expenses, tax implications, and long-term financial planning. This chapter explores comprehensive strategies for managing finances effectively as a remote worker, delving into budgeting techniques, ways to save on expenses, and building financial resilience.

Understanding Your Financial Landscape

Managing finances as a remote worker requires an in-depth evaluation of your financial situation, encompassing income sources, expenses, and financial goals. Without the structure of a typical office environment, there is a higher risk of financial disorganization. To maintain control over your finances, it is crucial to understand your income streams, whether they come from salaries, freelance work, consulting fees, or other sources

(Jackson, 2021).

Evaluating Income Streams: Remote workers often have multiple sources of income, ranging from full-time salaries to side hustles or freelance projects. Diversifying income streams can benefit financial stability but also requires diligent tracking. Creating a spreadsheet or using financial software to monitor income from different sources helps ensure that all earnings are accounted for (Smith, 2022).

Setting Financial Goals: Clearly defining short—and long-term financial goals is vital. Short-term goals may include reducing credit card debt or saving for an upcoming purchase. In contrast, long-term goals might focus on retirement savings, home ownership, or building a substantial emergency fund (Anderson, 2020).

Budgeting Basics

A well-crafted budget is the cornerstone of effective financial management, allowing remote workers to allocate income towards various financial priorities. A successful budget should account for both fixed and variable costs:

Fixed Costs: These are recurring expenses like rent/mortgage payments, utilities, internet service, and insurance—critical components for a functional remote work setup. Consider incorporating loan payments, subscriptions, and other obligatory payments into this category (Johnson, 2019).

Variable Costs: These expenses fluctuate month-to-month, including groceries, entertainment, dining out, and discretionary spending. Given the unpredictable nature of some of these costs, it is essential to monitor them closely and adjust as necessary (Thomas, 2023).

Tools for Budgeting

Several budgeting tools can help remote workers track spending, manage finances, and set goals. Consider the following:

Mint: This free tool allows users to link accounts, track spending, categorize expenses, and create goals. Mint's visual approach makes it easy to identify spending patterns and areas where adjustments are needed (Sullivan, 2021).

YNAB (You Need A Budget): YNAB follows a proactive approach to budgeting, helping users allocate income to specific expenses and savings categories. It emphasizes "giving every dollar a job" and encourages users to build savings while reducing unnecessary spending (Miller, 2020).

Spreadsheet Systems: For those who prefer a manual approach, creating spreadsheets in Excel or Google Sheets provides a customizable way to manage budgets. This method allows for a personalized structure that can be adapted to meet specific needs (Davis, 2022).

Managing Expenses in a Remote Environment

Remote workers often encounter new costs previously covered by employers, such as home office setups, technology upgrades, and utility costs. Here is how to manage these expenses:

Home Office Setup Costs

Setting up a productive home office can be costly, requiring ergonomic furniture, computers, software, and other equipment investments. While these initial expenses may seem overwhelming, they are necessary investments in long-term productivity (Peters, 2021).

Furniture and Equipment: For better ergonomics, invest in a comfortable chair, a suitable desk, and an additional monitor. While these items can be expensive, many employers offer stipends for home office setups, making it worthwhile to explore company benefits before purchasing (Brown, 2023).

Technology Upgrades: Reliable internet service, a good laptop, and relevant software are essential for remote work. Depending on your field, you may need additional tools, such as graphic design software, virtual meeting equipment, or collaborative platforms (Williams, 2020).

Tax Deductions: Certain home office expenses can be claimed as tax deductions for those eligible. The IRS allows deductions for a portion of the home used exclusively for work. To maximize deductions, keep detailed records of home office purchases, internet bills, and utilities (IRS, 2022).

Understanding Tax Implications
Remote work can complicate tax situations, particularly for individuals working across state lines or in different countries. Understanding the tax regulations applicable to your situation is essential for accurate reporting and maximizing deductions.

State and Local Taxes: Tax obligations can vary depending on where you live and work. For example, you might live in one state but work for a company headquartered in another. You may sometimes be required to file taxes in multiple states. Staying informed about local tax regulations and seeking advice from tax professionals can help avoid surprises (Fischer, 2021).

International Tax Implications: If you work remotely for a company based in another country, you may be subject to double taxation—paying taxes in both your home country and the country of your employer. Reviewing tax treaties between countries and consulting with international tax experts can guide in these complex situations (Global et al., 2021).

Cost-Saving Strategies for Remote Workers

Remote work offers several cost-saving opportunities that can contribute to overall financial well-being. Here are some strategies to reduce expenses:

Saving on Commuting Costs
A significant benefit of remote work is the elimination of commuting expenses, including gas, public transportation, parking, and vehicle maintenance. According to Global Workplace Analytics, remote workers can save an average

of $4,000 annually by avoiding commuting costs (Global et al., 2021). Redirecting these savings into a dedicated savings account or investment fund can help build long-term financial security.

Maximizing Home Office Deductions

As noted earlier, establishing a home office can lead to valuable tax deductions. Remote workers should keep thorough records of expenses related to their home office, such as:

Utility Bills: Proportional deductions can be claimed for utilities like electricity and heating, provided the space is exclusively used for work (IRS, 2022).

Internet Costs: Given the necessity of the Internet for remote work, a percentage of Internet expenses can also be deducted (Sullivan, 2021).

Equipment Depreciation: Items like computers, monitors, and desks may qualify for depreciation deductions (Brown, 2023).

Optimizing Remote Work Benefits

Many companies have started offering tailored benefits for remote employees. Here is how to make the most of these offerings:

Home Office Stipends: Some companies provide stipends for home office setups, covering expenses like furniture, equipment, or internet upgrades (Fischer, 2021).

Wellness Programs: Remote work can blur the lines between personal and professional life, potentially leading to burnout. Many organizations offer wellness programs that include mental health support, fitness stipends, and virtual wellness classes to encourage a balanced lifestyle (Williams, 2020).

Building Financial Security as a Remote Worker

Long-term financial stability is essential for peace of mind and preparing for uncertainties. Here are key strategies to build resilience:

Emergency Funds
An emergency fund is a financial safety net during income disruption or unexpected expenses. Financial experts recommend setting aside three to six months of living expenses in a separate, easily accessible savings account. This reserve provides security during job transitions or economic downturns (Anderson, 2020).

Automating Savings
Consider automating transfers from your checking to savings accounts to build savings effectively. Automating deposits ensures consistent growth without relying on willpower alone (Davis, 2022).

Investing in Personal Development
Continuous learning is crucial in the evolving remote work environment. Investing in courses, certifications, or skills training enhances career prospects and boosts earning potential (Jackson, 2021).

Real-World Example: Sarah's Financial Journey

Sarah, a graphic designer, transitioned to remote work two years ago. Initially, she needed help with managing expenses and understanding tax deductions. Realizing the importance of upskilling, she enrolled in an online UX/UI design course. This investment expanded her skills and increased her income by 30% (Thomas, 2023). Sarah's story highlights the potential of combining financial discipline with personal development.

As remote work redefines employment, sound financial planning is critical to thriving in this new work environment. By managing budgets, optimizing expenses, and building financial security, remote workers can leverage the benefits of remote work while minimizing risks. These principles foster personal well-being and a more prosperous future in an evolving work culture.

References

- Anderson, M. (2020). *Financial Strategies for the New Age Worker*. New York: Finance Press.
- Brown, R. (2023). *The Home Office Setup Guide*. Chicago: WorkSmart Publishers.
- Davis, L. (2022). *Budgeting for Freelancers and Remote Workers*. Boston: FinanceWorks Inc.
- Fischer, S. (2021). "Remote Work and State Tax Implications." *Tax Journal*, 34(4), 45–58.
- Global Workplace Analytics. (2021). *Cost of Employee Turnover*. Retrieved from Global Workplace Analytics
- IRS. (2022). "Home Office Deduction for Self-Employed Individuals." *IRS.gov*. Retrieved from IRS
- Jackson, T. (2021). *Remote Income Management*. Los Angeles: Future Finance Books.
- Johnson, A. (2019). *Personal Finance for Independent Workers*. Dallas: Budget Books.
- Miller, C. (2020). "How YNAB Can Help Remote Workers." *Personal Finance Weekly*, 12(8), 67–71.
- Peters, J. (2021). *Office Ergonomics for the Remote Worker*. San Francisco: HealthWise Publications.
- Smith, K. (2022). "Managing Diverse Income Streams as a Freelancer." *Entrepreneurial Finance*, 20(2), 32–41.
- Sullivan, N. (2021). *Digital Finance Tools for Remote Work*. Philadelphia: TechFin Publishers.
- Thomas, R. (2023). *Upskilling for Financial Growth*. Seattle: Skills Inc.
- Williams, L. (2020). *Remote Wellness Strategies*. Miami: Well-Being Press.

CHAPTER 12: NAVIGATING REMOTE JOB MARKETS AND INTERVIEWS

In today's rapidly evolving work environment, remote job markets have grown exponentially, driven by the increased demand for flexible work arrangements. As more companies adopt remote and hybrid work models, job seekers must adapt their strategies for finding, applying for, and succeeding in remote roles. This chapter delves into the complexities of navigating remote job markets, mastering virtual interviews, and negotiating offers to secure the best opportunities in the digital age.

Exploring Remote Job Markets

Finding remote job opportunities requires a different approach compared to traditional job searches. The remote job market is broad, spanning various industries and roles. To effectively explore this landscape, you must leverage specialized job boards, network within remote work communities, and optimize your online presence.

Utilizing Specialized Remote Job Boards

One of the most effective ways to discover remote job opportunities is by using job boards explicitly dedicated to remote work. These platforms offer comprehensive resources beyond job listings, such as company reviews, salary information, and remote work trends.

We Work Remotely: This job board is a leading platform that caters exclusively to remote positions across multiple industries, including technology, marketing, customer support, and more. It allows job seekers to filter roles based on categories, which makes the search process more efficient (We Work Remotely, 2021).

Remote.co: Another popular resource, Remote. Co offers curated listings of remote jobs, ranging from entry-level to executive roles. It also provides tips for remote workers, such as articles on work-life balance, managing time zones, and maintaining productivity.

FlexJobs: FlexJobs offers a wide range of remote and flexible job opportunities. While it requires a subscription fee, FlexJobs screens all job listings for legitimacy, reducing the likelihood of encountering scams (FlexJobs, 2020).

AngelList: For those interested in remote work within the startup ecosystem, AngelList is an excellent platform. It features remote job opportunities at startups worldwide, providing a unique space to explore roles in emerging industries.

Real-World Example: John's Remote Job Search

John, a software developer, transitioned from a traditional office-based role to a freelance remote position by strategically using remote job boards. He set up daily job alerts for specific keywords related to his skills and found roles aligned with his career goals. John's approach allowed him to secure a lucrative contract, demonstrating how effective targeted job searches can be in the remote landscape.

Networking in Remote Communities

Networking is essential to any job search, and remote work is no exception. Engaging with online communities and professional networks can significantly enhance your remote job search by providing access to job leads, insider information about company cultures, and potential referrals.

LinkedIn Groups: Join industry-specific LinkedIn groups where remote work discussions are expected. Actively participate in conversations by sharing insights, asking questions, and offering help to others. This engagement increases visibility and positions you as an active member of the remote work community.

Industry-Specific Forums: Platforms like GitHub (for tech professionals), Behance (for creatives), and Dribbble (for designers) offer opportunities to connect with like-minded professionals, showcase portfolios, and discuss job opportunities. These forums can lead to collaborations, referrals, and direct connections with hiring managers.

Remote Work Events and Meetups: Virtual meetups and webinars dedicated to remote work topics are becoming increasingly popular. Events hosted by companies like Remote.com and Remote-First Institute provide opportunities to network with industry leaders, learn about remote work trends, and gain insights into job openings.

Leveraging Social Media for Job Search
Social media has become a powerful tool for job hunting, especially in the remote work sector. Platforms like LinkedIn and Twitter allow job seekers to interact directly with companies, recruiters, and employees.

- **LinkedIn Strategies**: Optimize your LinkedIn profile for remote job searches. Use relevant keywords in your headline and summary to appear in recruiter searches. Engage with company posts by liking, commenting, and sharing to increase your visibility.

- **Twitter Hashtags**: Using hashtags like #RemoteJobs, #RemoteWork, or #WorkFromHome can help you discover job postings and connect with recruiters. Following industry leaders and participating in Twitter chats related to remote work can also increase your chances of finding remote opportunities.
- **Creating a Personal Brand**: Building a solid brand on platforms like LinkedIn, Twitter, and personal websites can help establish credibility. Share insights, write articles, and showcase your skills to attract attention from recruiters looking for remote talent.

Mastering Virtual Interviews

Virtual interviews have become a standard practice in remote hiring processes. While similar to traditional interviews in some ways, virtual interviews require additional preparation to handle the nuances of the digital format effectively.

Preparing for Online Interviews

Preparation is the key to excelling in virtual interviews. Candidates should take specific steps to ensure a seamless experience:

Conduct a Tech Check: Test your internet connection, camera, and microphone before the interview. Using reliable video conferencing software (like Zoom, Microsoft Teams, or Google Meet) is essential for a smooth interaction. Make sure your background is tidy and professional, as this creates a positive impression.

Dress Appropriately: While you might be interviewing from home, dressing professionally—at least from the waist up—demonstrates respect for the process and helps set a formal tone.

Minimize Distractions: Choose a quiet, well-lit space for your interview. Inform family members or roommates about your interview time to avoid interruptions—silence notifications on your computer and phone to maintain focus.

Real-World Example: Emily's Interview Preparation

Emily, a marketing professional, experienced technical issues during her first virtual interview, causing her to feel flustered. After that experience, she conducted tech checks before every interview, ensuring her equipment worked correctly. This change led to seamless interviews and eventually helped her land her dream remote job. Emily's story underscores the importance of technical preparation for successful virtual interviews.

Developing Effective Communication Skills

Communication is crucial in virtual interviews. Here are ways to enhance communication during online interviews:

- **Active Listening**: Show that you are actively engaged by nodding, maintaining eye contact, and responding promptly. Avoid interrupting the interviewer, and use verbal cues like "I see" or "That is a great point" to show attentiveness.
- **Clear and Concise Responses**: Practice answering common interview questions with clear, concise responses. Use the STAR method (Situation, Task, Action, Result) to structure answers to behavioral questions, providing specific examples of your experiences.
- **Ask Thoughtful Questions**: Prepare insightful questions for the interviewer, focusing on topics like remote team dynamics, communication tools used by the company, and expectations for remote employees. This demonstrates genuine interest and helps you evaluate the company's fit for your work style.

Negotiating Remote Job Offers

Once you have received a job offer, negotiation is the next crucial step. Negotiating remotely requires clear communication, an understanding of industry standards, and confidence in your value.

Understanding Salary Expectations

Before entering negotiations, research typical salary ranges for similar roles in your industry and geographical location. Resources like Glassdoor, PayScale, and Salary.com provide insights into salary data, helping you establish a reasonable target.

Know Your Worth: Be prepared to articulate your value based on skills, experience, and accomplishments. Use data from salary research to support your case when discussing compensation. For example, if you find that the average salary for your role is 15% higher than what was offered, present this information factually to the employer.

Highlight Unique Skills: If you have specific skills that are highly sought after—like fluency in multiple languages, advanced technical expertise, or certifications in project management—emphasize these during negotiations to justify a higher salary request.

Considering Benefits Beyond Salary

Negotiating remote job offers involves more than just salary discussions. The overall compensation package, including benefits like flexible work hours, wellness programs, and professional development opportunities, is equally important.

Flexible Work Hours: Remote work offers the advantage of flexibility. Discuss your preferred working hours to ensure they align with the company's expectations.

Professional Development: Many companies provide training, courses, or certification stipends. Requesting a professional development budget can be a valuable addition to your compensation package and contribute to long-term career growth.

Wellness Programs: With the rise of remote work, many employers offer wellness benefits like mental health support, gym memberships, or meditation app subscriptions. Consider negotiating these perks as part of the overall package.

Building Confidence in Negotiations

Negotiating can be intimidating, especially when done remotely. However, practicing with friends and mentors, or even through role-playing exercises, can help build confidence.

Role-Playing Scenarios: Simulating negotiation conversations can help you articulate your needs and respond to objections effectively. Practicing this skill prepares you for negotiations and increases your chances of a positive outcome.

Documenting Achievements: Before negotiations, create a document outlining your past achievements, contributions, and skills. This will boost your confidence and provide tangible evidence to support your requests.

Real-World Example: Sarah's Salary Negotiation

When Sarah received a job offer for a remote project management role, she felt anxious about negotiating her salary. After practicing with a mentor, she confidently requested a salary increase based on her research. The employer appreciated her preparation and agreed to a higher salary. Sarah's experience highlights the importance of preparation and self-advocacy in negotiations.

As remote job markets expand, navigating them successfully requires strategic approaches to finding opportunities, excelling in interviews, and negotiating offers. By leveraging specialized job boards, networking effectively, and mastering virtual interview techniques, job seekers can position themselves for success in the competitive landscape of remote work. Moreover, understanding salary expectations and the overall benefits of a job offer empowers individuals to make informed decisions that align with their professional goals and personal values. As the remote work landscape evolves, these skills and strategies will be essential for long-term career growth and fulfillment.

References

- FlexJobs. (2020). *The Guide to Finding Remote Work*. Retrieved from FlexJobs.
- Glassdoor. (2021). *How to Negotiate Your Salary*. Retrieved from Glassdoor.
- LinkedIn. (2021). *The Ultimate Guide to Remote Work*. Retrieved from LinkedIn.
- PayScale. (2022). *Remote Work Salary Guide*. Retrieved from PayScale.
- We Work Remotely. (2021). *Top Remote Job Boards*. Retrieved from We Work Remotely.

CHAPTER 13: SELF-CARE STRATEGIES FOR REMOTE SUCCESS

Maintaining a healthy work-life balance is crucial in the ever-evolving landscape of remote work. While remote work offers flexibility and convenience, it can blur the lines between professional responsibilities and personal well-being. This chapter delves into self-care strategies for sustaining productivity, mental health, and happiness in a remote work environment. We will explore the importance of prioritizing self-care, building a solid support network, and maintaining motivation for long-term success.

Understanding Self-Care in a Remote Context

Self-care is more than just a trendy concept; it is a vital practice for enhancing overall well-being and productivity. In a remote setting, where the boundaries between work and personal life can quickly become blurred, prioritizing self-care is essential. A study published in the *Journal of Occupational Health Psychology* shows that individuals who engage in regular self-care activities report lower stress levels, improved job performance, and greater job satisfaction (Sonnentag & Fritz, 2015).

The Different Dimensions of Self-Care

Remote workers often focus solely on physical well-being, but proper self-care encompasses several dimensions:

Physical Well-Being: Incorporating exercise, a balanced diet, and adequate sleep is critical. Even in short bursts, regular physical activity can boost mood, increase energy levels, and reduce stress (Rebar et al., 2015). Maintaining healthy eating habits and avoiding relying solely on convenience foods that lack nutrition is essential.

Emotional Well-Being: Managing emotions in a remote setting can be challenging, as workers might experience isolation, stress, or frustration. Journaling, engaging in hobbies, and practicing mindfulness are effective ways to process emotions healthily.

Social Well-Being: Fostering connections with family, friends, and colleagues is crucial for mental health. Remote work can be isolating, so regular virtual or in-person interactions are necessary for maintaining a sense of community.

Professional Well-Being: Continuing education, skill development, and setting clear professional boundaries contribute to career satisfaction. Investing in personal growth through online courses, certifications, or webinars can enhance job performance and increase confidence.

Why Self-Care Matters in Remote Work

Refrain from self-care to avoid burnout, decreased motivation, and dissatisfaction with remote work. The blurred lines between work and personal time can make it difficult to "switch off," leading to overworking and potential mental fatigue. Implementing self-care strategies promotes better mental health and improves productivity, as individuals who feel well-rested and emotionally balanced are more likely to perform efficiently.

Incorporating Wellness Routines into Your Workday

Integrating wellness routines into your daily schedule can enhance mental and physical health. Here are some strategies for incorporating self-care into your remote work routine:

1. Regular Exercise

Physical activity is one of the most effective ways to boost mental health and energy levels. Exercise releases endorphins, which are natural mood lifters. Incorporating exercise into your day does not necessarily require a gym membership; many home-based options fit a remote worker's schedule:

- **Home Workouts**: Set aside time for a 20–30 minute workout session in your living room, using apps like Nike Training Club or YouTube channels dedicated to at-home fitness. Workouts can include bodyweight exercises, yoga, or dance routines.
- **Walking Breaks**: Taking short walks outdoors during breaks provides physical activity and a mental reset, which can boost creativity and focus. A brisk 10-minute walk can improve mood and reduce anxiety (Rebar et al., 2015).
- **Desk Exercises**: For tight schedules, stretching or desk exercises can relieve tension and increase circulation. Simple neck, shoulders, and back stretches can reduce discomfort and enhance working comfort.

2. Mindful Breaks

Mindfulness is a powerful tool for reducing stress and improving focus. Incorporating mindfulness practices into your routine can help create a sense of calm and enhance mental clarity:

- **Deep Breathing Exercises**: Set aside a few minutes during breaks to practice deep breathing. This simple technique can lower stress and increase focus.

- **Meditation**: Use meditation apps like Headspace or Calm to guide you through short, daily sessions. Research in *Mindfulness* has shown that even brief mindfulness practices can enhance cognitive flexibility and improve attention (Zeidan et al., 2010).
- **Progressive Muscle Relaxation (PMR)**: PMR involves tensing and releasing different muscle groups, promoting relaxation and reducing anxiety. Integrating PMR into a daily routine can significantly lower stress levels.

3. Nutrition and Hydration

Eating well-balanced meals and staying hydrated are crucial for maintaining energy levels and cognitive function. Remote workers might find it easy to snack throughout the day or skip meals due to workload, but these habits can negatively impact health and productivity.

- **Meal Planning**: Planning meals in advance can help ensure a balanced diet. When preparing meals, focus on nutrient-rich foods such as fruits, vegetables, lean proteins, and whole grains.
- **Healthy Snacks**: Keep healthy snacks like nuts, fruit, or yogurt on hand. Avoid sugary snacks and energy drinks, which can cause energy crashes.
- **Hydration**: Dehydration can lead to decreased focus and energy. Keep a water bottle at your desk, and aim to drink at least eight glasses of water daily.

4. Sleep Hygiene

Adequate sleep is essential for cognitive function and overall health. Poor sleep can lead to irritability, lack of focus, and decreased productivity. Establishing good sleep hygiene can improve sleep quality and enhance well-being:

- **Create a Sleep Routine**: Go to bed and wake up simultaneously every day, even on weekends.

Consistency helps regulate your body's internal clock and improves sleep quality (Walker, 2017).
- **Optimize Your Sleep Environment**: Ensure your bedroom is dark, quiet, and at a comfortable temperature. Consider using earplugs, a sleep mask, or white noise machines if needed.
- **Limit Screen Time Before Bed**: Screens emit blue light, which can interfere with sleep. Avoid using electronic devices at least 30 minutes before bedtime to promote better sleep.

Creating a Support Network

Building and maintaining a solid support network is crucial for emotional resilience and personal growth, especially in remote work environments with limited face-to-face interactions.

The Importance of Connection

Human connection is vital for combating isolation and promoting a sense of belonging. Research indicates that social support is critical in reducing stress, increasing life satisfaction, and enhancing mental health (Cohen & Wills, 1985).

Engaging with Family and Friends

Maintaining personal relationships is essential for emotional well-being. Here are some strategies to keep connections strong:

Regular Communication: Schedule regular video calls or phone conversations with loved ones. Virtual gatherings, such as online game nights or movie streaming parties, can add fun to interactions and strengthen bonds.

Share Experiences: Openly share your feelings and experiences with those close to you. Expressing emotions can be cathartic and help you gain perspective on work-related stress.

Finding Professional Mentors

In addition to personal connections, developing professional relationships is equally essential for career growth and motivation.

Seek Guidance: Find mentors who can offer advice, provide insights, and support your career development. Mentorship can be formal (through workplace programs) or informal (through industry groups).

Network Virtually: Join online professional groups or forums related to your field. Platforms like LinkedIn, Slack communities, and industry-specific forums offer opportunities to engage with peers and mentors, providing guidance and support.

Maintaining Motivation

Staying motivated in remote work requires proactive strategies to maintain focus and drive. Here are some practical ways to sustain motivation:

Strategies for Staying Driven

Set Clear Goals: Establishing achievable goals helps maintain focus and direction. Set short-term goals (e.g., completing a project milestone) and long-term goals (e.g., earning a certification). Break these goals into smaller tasks to create a sense of progress and accomplishment (Locke & Latham, 2002).

Create a Structured Routine: A structured daily routine can help establish boundaries between work and personal time, creating a sense of normalcy. Include regular work hours, breaks, and dedicated time for personal activities. According to a survey by FlexJobs, 80% of remote workers find that having a set routine boosts productivity (FlexJobs, 2020).

Celebrate Small Wins: Recognizing and celebrating achievements, no matter how minor, can boost morale and motivation. Consider rewarding yourself with small treats, like taking a longer break or enjoying a favorite snack.

Engage in Continuous Learning: Taking online courses, attending webinars, and reading industry-related materials can help keep you engaged and motivated. Learning new skills enhances your resume and fosters personal growth.

Limit Distractions: Identify potential distractions in your home environment and implement strategies to minimize them. This could mean setting specific work hours, using apps that block distracting websites, or creating a dedicated workspace that signals it is time to focus.

Self-care is a luxury and a necessity for thriving in a remote work environment. By prioritizing wellness, fostering connections, and maintaining motivation, remote workers can navigate the unique challenges of their roles while ensuring their well-being. Implementing these strategies can lead to increased productivity, greater job satisfaction, and an improved overall quality of life. Remember, self-care is an ongoing process that requires conscious effort and regular adjustment as personal and professional needs evolve.

References

- Cohen, S., & Wills, T. A. (1985). Stress, social support, and the buffering hypothesis. *Psychological Bulletin*, 98(2), 310-357.
- FlexJobs. (2020). The Benefits of Working Remotely: 2020. Retrieved from FlexJobs.
- Locke, E. A., & Latham, G. P. (2002). Building a practically functional theory of goal setting and task motivation: A 35-year odyssey. *American Psychologist*, 57(9), 705–717.
- Rebar, A. L., Stanton, R., Geard, D., Short, C., Duncan, M. J., & Vandelanotte, C. (2015). A meta-meta-analysis of the effect of physical activity on depression and anxiety. *Health Psychology Review*, 9(3), 341–355.
- Sonnentag, S., & Fritz, C. (2015). Recovery from job stress: The stressor-recovery model. *The Cambridge Handbook of Workplace Training and Employee Development* (pp. 325-348). Cambridge University Press.

- Walker, A. (2017). *Why We Sleep: Unlocking the Power of Sleep and Dreams*. Scribner.
- Zeidan, F., Johnson, S. K., Diamond, B. J., David, A. B., & Goolkasian, P. (2010). Mindfulness meditation improves cognition: Evidence of brief mental training. *Consciousness and Cognition*, 19(2), 597-605.

CHAPTER 14: OVERCOMING COMMON REMOTE WORK CHALLENGES

In the landscape of remote work, challenges can loom as large as the opportunities. While remote work offers flexibility, comfort, and convenience, it also brings about specific hurdles that can threaten productivity, connection, and mental well-being. This chapter will explore three common challenges remote workers face—handling isolation and loneliness, managing tech fatigue, and dealing with conflicts. Remote workers can navigate these challenges resiliently and achieve long-term success by employing thoughtful strategies.

Handling Isolation and Loneliness

Understanding the Emotional Landscape

For many, the shift to remote work has been accompanied by a sense of isolation that can feel overwhelming. The absence of daily in-person interactions can lead to feelings of disconnection. A study by Buffer found that 20% of remote workers cite loneliness as their biggest struggle (Buffer, 2021). Without spontaneous conversations at the coffee machine or casual banter during lunch breaks, many remote workers experience a void in their social lives that can negatively impact mental health.

Loneliness and isolation can affect remote workers differently based on personality, work culture, and communication dynamics. Extroverts, for example, may feel more isolated without regular social interactions, while introverts might find remote work more comfortable but still need more connection over time.

The Psychological Impact of Loneliness

Loneliness affects emotional well-being and has physical and cognitive consequences. Studies have linked chronic loneliness to higher levels of stress, anxiety, and even health issues such as high blood pressure and weakened immune response (Cacioppo et al., 2015). Additionally, prolonged isolation can decrease job satisfaction, reduce motivation, and hinder professional growth, as a lack of meaningful interaction can result in reduced engagement and collaboration.

Strategies for Connection

To combat isolation, it is vital to create intentional social connections. Here are some strategies that can help remote workers stay connected:

Schedule Regular Check-Ins:
Set aside time for virtual coffee breaks or informal chats with colleagues. While work meetings are essential, casual, non-work-related conversations help foster camaraderie and build relationships.

Consider implementing "virtual water cooler" moments—brief, spontaneous video calls replicating casual office interactions. Tools like Donut, which pairs colleagues for random video calls, can facilitate these moments.

Leverage Social Media and Networking Platforms:
Engage actively in professional communities on LinkedIn, Slack, or industry-specific forums. Sharing insights, asking questions, and participating in discussions can create a sense of belonging.

Explore LinkedIn Groups related to your industry or interests, participate in discussions, and contribute by sharing articles or personal experiences. This will enhance your professional network and promote engagement.

Participate in Team-Building Activities:
Advocate for virtual team-building exercises, such as online trivia games, escape rooms, or creative challenges that allow team members to engage in a relaxed manner. These activities can break the monotony of work meetings and foster a sense of fun and teamwork.

Encourage virtual retreats or workshops where teams can learn, share, and bond over non-work-related topics, such as cooking classes, art sessions, or wellness programs.

Join Remote Work Groups:
Explore online groups or forums dedicated to remote work, such as r/remotework on Reddit or Slack channels for remote professionals. These platforms can offer support, advice, and camaraderie.

Attend virtual meetups or conferences relevant to your industry. Platforms like Eventbrite and Meetup offer many virtual events that allow remote workers to network and learn from peers.

Cultivate Relationships Outside of Work:
Make time for friends and family, even scheduling regular virtual get-togethers. Sharing activities like watching movies together online or playing virtual games can strengthen bonds.

Volunteering for remote opportunities, such as mentoring, teaching, or participating in community projects, can add a sense of purpose and connection.

The Power of Vulnerability

It is important to remember that feelings of loneliness or isolation are common in remote work settings. Sharing these emotions with colleagues can foster an environment of openness and vulnerability, leading to deeper connections. When individuals acknowledge their struggles, it normalizes the conversation around mental health and emotional well-being in the workplace, making it easier for others to open up as well.

Managing Tech Fatigue

Recognizing the Impact of Digital Overload

While technology is essential for remote work, it can also lead to a phenomenon known as "tech fatigue" or "digital burnout." Prolonged screen time and constant connectivity can cause physical discomfort, decreased productivity, and mental exhaustion. According to the American Psychological Association, remote workers experience higher stress levels related to technology use than their in-office counterparts (American Psychological Association, 2020).

Digital overload occurs when digital devices and platforms continuously overwhelm an individual's mental capacity, leading to exhaustion. Symptoms can include eye strain, headaches, irritability, and reduced concentration. Additionally, the blurring of work and personal life—fueled by constant notifications and the expectation of being "always on"—can contribute to anxiety and mental fatigue.

Strategies to Combat Tech Fatigue

Here are practical strategies to manage tech fatigue and promote well-being in a digital environment:

Implement the 20-20-20 Rule:

To reduce eye strain, follow the 20-20-20 rule: For every 20 minutes of screen time, look at something 20 feet away for at least 20 seconds. This simple technique can help alleviate digital eye strain and improve focus throughout the workday.

Establish Tech-Free Zones:

Designate areas in your home that are free from screens. Whether it is a cozy reading nook, a spot for mindfulness, or an outdoor space, having tech-free zones allows for mental breaks from digital engagement.

Consider creating a "tech curfew" by setting a specific time in the evening when you stop using electronic devices. This will not only help reduce tech fatigue but also improve sleep quality.

Schedule Regular Breaks:

Taking breaks throughout the workday is essential to maintain focus and energy. Use techniques like the Pomodoro method, which encourages 25 minutes of focused work followed by a 5-minute break, to create a rhythm that minimizes mental fatigue. Step away from screens during breaks and engage in non-digital activities like stretching, reading a physical book, or walking. This can help refresh your mind and reduce stress.

Limit Notifications:

Reduce distractions by turning off non-essential notifications on your computer and mobile devices. Tools like Focus@Will and Freedom can help block distracting websites or apps, allowing for uninterrupted work time.

Establish "deep work" periods when all notifications are silenced. This will enable you to focus entirely on tasks without digital interruptions.

Practice Digital Detox:

At the end of each workday, take a break from technology. Engage in offline activities like cooking, gardening, exercising, or hobbies that do not involve screens.

Consider dedicating one day a week as a "digital detox day," where you minimize technology use as much as possible to reset and recharge.

Embracing Mindful Tech Usage

Approaching technology use with mindfulness can improve the remote work experience. Being intentional about when, where, and how technology is used fosters a healthier work-life balance and enhances overall productivity. Mindful tech usage can help remote workers stay present, reduce stress, and avoid burnout.

Dealing with Remote Work Conflicts

The Nature of Remote Conflicts

Conflicts in remote work often arise from misunderstandings, miscommunications, and the lack of non-verbal cues that typically aid in interpersonal interactions. Face-to-face communication can be more accessible in terms of interpreting tone, intention, or body language, which can lead to misinterpretations. According to the Society for Human Resource Management (SHRM), remote work settings can exacerbate conflicts due to communication barriers (SHRM, 2020).

Conflicts in remote environments can manifest in various forms, including:

Misunderstandings: Misinterpreting written messages due to lack of context or tone can cause confusion and frustration.

Delayed Responses: In asynchronous communication, delayed responses can create tension or anxiety, as team members may perceive the delay as a lack of interest or urgency.

Cultural Differences: Remote teams often include members from diverse cultural backgrounds, leading to differences in communication styles, work habits, and expectations.

Strategies for Conflict Resolution
Utilize Communication Tools Effectively:
Leverage video calls and chats to address misunderstandings promptly. Visual cues and tone of voice can convey meanings that written communication cannot. Use platforms like Zoom, Microsoft Teams, or Slack for real-time discussions that can help clarify issues.

Use emojis and GIFs cautiously in written communication. They can be misinterpreted across cultures or viewed as unprofessional. Clear and straightforward language is generally more effective.

Practice Active Listening:
When conflicts arise, ensure that all parties feel heard. Use active listening techniques, such as paraphrasing the other person's words, to demonstrate that their perspective is valued. Avoid interrupting and allow others to express themselves fully before responding.

Address Issues Early:
>Do not let conflicts simmer. Address issues as soon as they arise to prevent escalation. Proactively resolving conflict shows emotional intelligence and fosters a collaborative work environment.

Emphasize Empathy:
>Approach conflicts with empathy and understanding. Recognize that everyone is navigating the complexities of remote work, and extend grace to colleagues dealing with personal or professional challenges. This empathetic approach can help de-escalate tensions and build trust.

Involve a Mediator if Necessary:
>If conflicts cannot be resolved internally, consider involving a neutral third party to mediate the discussion.

This could be an HR representative, a team leader, or an external mediator who can facilitate productive dialogue and help resolve.

Fostering a Positive Conflict Resolution Culture

Building a culture that embraces open communication and conflict resolution can transform remote work environments. Teams that encourage transparent discussions and emphasize collaboration can create a more supportive atmosphere where individuals feel empowered to express their concerns.

Regular Team Meetings: Hold regular meetings that allow team members to voice concerns and discuss any issues openly. This proactive approach can prevent conflicts from escalating.

Establish Clear Communication Guidelines: Define how and when communication should occur within the team. Clarifying expectations around response times, communication channels, and meeting formats can reduce misunderstandings.

Promote a Feedback Culture: Encourage feedback among team members, fostering a culture where constructive criticism is welcomed and used for growth.

Overcoming common remote work challenges requires a proactive approach and a commitment to personal and professional growth. By prioritizing social connections, managing tech fatigue, and developing effective conflict resolution strategies, remote workers can navigate the complexities of their roles and thrive in a flexible work environment. In doing so, they can cultivate their careers and well-being in the ever-changing landscape of remote work.

References

- American Psychological Association. (2020). *Stress in America: Stress and Technology*. Retrieved from APA.
- Buffer. (2021). *State of Remote Work 2021*. Retrieved

from Buffer.
- Cacioppo, J. T., Cacioppo, S., & Boomsma, D. I. (2015). Evolutionary mechanisms for loneliness. *Cognition and Emotion*, 29(1), 3-18.
- Society for Human Resource Management (SHRM). (2020). *Managing Remote Workers: Best Practices for HR*. Retrieved from SHRM.

CHAPTER 15: CREATING YOUR PERSONALIZED REMOTE WORK PLAN

As remote work solidifies its place in the professional landscape, creating a personalized remote work plan becomes increasingly vital. A tailored approach enhances productivity and aligns work habits with career aspirations. This chapter will explore how to craft a remote work blueprint that suits your unique needs, build long-term success by aligning your efforts with career goals, and develop a practical roadmap to continuously refine and adapt your remote work strategy.

Crafting Your Remote Work Blueprint

Creating a personalized remote work blueprint involves understanding your work style, setting clear goals, and establishing effective routines. Every remote worker has different needs—some thrive in a structured environment, while others flourish more flexibly. The key is to design a plan that aligns with your natural preferences while addressing professional responsibilities.

Step 1: Assess Your Work Style

The first step in crafting your remote work blueprint is to assess your work style. This involves evaluating your peak productivity periods, preferred working methods, and the environment in which you perform best.

Identify Your Peak Hours: Take note of when you feel most energetic and focused throughout the day. Are you a morning person who tackles tasks efficiently at sunrise, or are you more productive during afternoon or evening hours? Aligning work tasks with your peak productivity times can significantly boost performance. According to a study in the *Journal of Applied Psychology*, individuals who schedule tasks during their most productive hours experience up to a 15% increase in efficiency and output (Huang et al., 2015).

Understand Your Work Preferences: Do you prefer deep work —long, uninterrupted periods of focused tasks—or do you perform better in short, concentrated bursts? Understanding whether you work best with uninterrupted blocks or frequent breaks can help you create a routine that maximizes productivity.

Analyze Your Working Environment: Reflect on the type of environment that helps you focus. Do you thrive in complete silence, or do you work better with some background noise? Experiment with different settings, such as using white noise, playing music, or having complete quiet, to find what works best for you.

Step 2: Set Clear Goals

Once you have assessed your work style, setting clear, achievable goals is the next step. Having well-defined objectives provides direction and helps you measure progress over time. Consider the following strategies for goal setting:

Use SMART Criteria: The SMART framework—Specific, Measurable, Achievable, Relevant, and Time-bound—is widely used for setting practical goals. For example, instead of setting a vague goal like "improve my skills," aim for a more specific target like "complete a certification course in my field by the end of Q2."

This specificity helps maintain focus and provides a clear metric for success.

Differentiate Short-Term and Long-Term Goals: Break down your goals into short-term and long-term categories. Short-term goals can include daily or weekly targets, such as finishing a project by the end of the week or attending a professional webinar. Long-term goals should align with your broader career aspirations, like earning a promotion within a year or transitioning to a new role.

Visualize Your Goals: Visualization is a powerful technique for goal achievement. Create a vision board or use digital tools like Trello or Asana to map your goals visually. Seeing your objectives displayed can enhance motivation and constantly remind you of what you are working toward.

Step 3: Establish Effective Routines

An intense routine is the backbone of any successful remote work plan. A consistent daily schedule boosts productivity and helps maintain a healthy work-life balance. Here is how to create an effective routine:

Time Blocking: Time blocking involves allocating specific hours for tasks. For instance, reserve the first two hours of your day for deep work, followed by a one-hour block for meetings or collaborative tasks. Research indicates that time blocking can increase focus by reducing multitasking and creating a predictable schedule (Mackenzie & O'Brien, 2018).

Incorporate Regular Breaks: Avoid burnout by scheduling regular breaks throughout your day. Techniques like the Pomodoro method, which encourages 25-minute work intervals followed by 5-minute breaks, can help maintain energy and prevent fatigue.

Set Boundaries: Establish clear boundaries between work and personal time. Communicate your work hours to colleagues, and avoid responding to work messages during off-hours. Creating a physical boundary—such as having a dedicated workspace—can also signal to your brain when it is time to work and when it is time to relax.

Step 4: Select the Right Tools

Choosing the right tools and technology is crucial for a successful remote work plan. Your digital tools should streamline workflows, enhance communication, and increase efficiency. Consider these categories of tools:

Project Management Tools: Platforms like Asana, Trello, and Monday.com allow you to organize tasks, set deadlines, and track progress. These tools are handy for remote teams, providing a centralized hub for collaboration and project updates.

Communication Tools: Effective communication is the foundation of remote work success. Use tools like Slack, Microsoft Teams, or Zoom for real-time messaging, video calls, and virtual meetings. Ensure you have a reliable video conferencing setup, including a good webcam and microphone, to maintain clear communication.

Productivity Enhancers: Tools like RescueTime, Focus@Will, and Notion can help you manage time, track productivity, and organize information. Research shows that effective use of productivity tools can increase job satisfaction and reduce stress (Morrison, 2020).

Building Long-Term Success

A personalized remote work plan should address immediate productivity and align with long-term career goals. Adopting strategies that support career advancement and personal development is essential to achieving sustained growth and success.

Aligning with Career Goals

Understanding your career aspirations is fundamental to creating a personalized remote work plan. Consider the following questions to align your work activities with your long-term goals:

What are your ultimate career aspirations? Reflect on where you see yourself in the next five or ten years. Do you aim to advance within your current organization, transition to a new field, or start your own business?

How can remote work support these goals? Consider how the flexibility of remote work can help you pursue additional education, build a side business, or develop new skills that align with your career path.

What steps can you take now to progress toward your goals? Identify specific actions, such as pursuing certifications, seeking leadership opportunities, or engaging in networking activities that will contribute to your long-term success.

Continuous Learning and Upskilling

Investing in continuous learning is crucial in the ever-evolving job market. Accessing online resources and training programs that can enhance your skills and career prospects is more accessible than ever in a remote work setting.

Identify In-Demand Skills: Research the most sought-after skills in your field. Are there technical skills, like coding or data analysis, that are becoming increasingly important? Or are soft skills, like communication or leadership, crucial for advancement?

Leverage Online Learning Platforms: Coursera, LinkedIn Learning, and Udemy offer courses catering to different skill levels and fields. Completing these courses enhances your skill set and adds credibility to your resume.

Pursue Certifications: Earning certifications in relevant areas can boost your professional profile and increase your competitiveness in the job market. Certifications in project management (like PMP), digital marketing, or IT (like AWS certification) can significantly enhance your career prospects.

Networking for Opportunities

Networking remains a vital component of career growth, even in remote settings. Building a solid professional network can open new opportunities, collaborations, and partnerships.

- **Use LinkedIn Effectively**: Update your LinkedIn profile to reflect your current role, skills, and career aspirations. Engage with content, share articles, and participate in discussions to increase visibility and demonstrate your expertise.
- **Attend Virtual Conferences**: Many industries host virtual conferences and events that allow professionals to network, learn, and exchange ideas. Attending these events can help you expand your network and stay updated on industry trends.
- **Engage in Online Communities**: Join online forums, Slack channels, or professional groups related to your field. Participating in these communities allows you to connect with like-minded professionals, seek advice, and explore new opportunities.

Seeking Feedback and Mentorship

Regular feedback is essential for personal and professional development. It provides insights into your strengths, areas for improvement, and progress toward your goals.

Request Feedback from Supervisors and Peers: Schedule regular check-ins with your manager to discuss performance, challenges, and areas for growth. Use this feedback to refine your work plan and make necessary adjustments.

Find a Mentor: Mentorship can be a powerful tool for career growth. A mentor can offer guidance, share experiences, and provide support as you navigate your career path. Seek mentors within your organization or through professional networks.

Your Remote Work Roadmap

Developing a remote work roadmap allows you to create a practical guide for refining and adapting your strategy over time. This roadmap should include actionable steps, timelines, and checkpoints to measure your progress.

Step 1: Set Milestones

Identify critical milestones that align with your goals. These could include completing a training program, reaching performance targets, or expanding your professional network. Breaking down larger goals into smaller, achievable milestones helps maintain motivation and provides a sense of accomplishment.

Short-Term Milestones: Examples include completing a course, achieving a weekly productivity target, or making a certain number of new professional connections within a month.

Long-term Milestones might involve earning a promotion, changing roles, or transitioning to a new industry. They require consistent effort and should be regularly evaluated.

Step 2: Review and Reflect

Regularly review your progress and reflect on what has worked well and what needs adjustment. Use the following methods to assess your progress:

Weekly Check-Ins: Dedicate time at the end of each week to reviewing your progress, assessing productivity, and identifying areas for improvement.

Quarterly Reflections: Every quarter, take a broader look at your goals and strategies. Are you meeting your productivity targets? Are your communication practices effective? Use this time to adjust your roadmap based on what is working and what is not.

Step 3: Stay Flexible

Flexibility is crucial in the dynamic landscape of remote work.

Be open to adjusting your plans as circumstances change. Whether adopting new technology, altering your schedule, or re-evaluating your goals, maintaining a flexible mindset enables you to navigate challenges effectively.

Adapt to New Tools: As new tools and technologies become available, be willing to explore and adopt those that can improve efficiency or communication.

Adjust Routines as Needed: Your personal and professional needs may change over time, so be ready to adjust your routines to maintain balance and productivity.

Step 4: Celebrate Achievements

As you reach milestones and achieve goals, take the time to celebrate your successes. Acknowledging accomplishments not only boosts motivation but also reinforces the importance of your efforts.

Personal Rewards: When you achieve a significant milestone, treat yourself to something special, such as a day off, a meal, or a new gadget.

Share Achievements with Colleagues: Sharing your successes with colleagues can foster a positive work environment and encourage others to celebrate their achievements.

Creating a personalized remote work plan is an empowering process that can significantly enhance your productivity and career growth. You can thrive in the remote work landscape by understanding your work style, setting clear goals, establishing routines, and aligning your approach with long-term aspirations. Remember, this journey is about working remotely and building a fulfilling and sustainable career that aligns with your values and ambitions. Embrace the flexibility and opportunities remote work offers, and let your personalized plan guide you to success.

References

- Huang, Y., Liu, Y., & Zhao, S. (2015). *Effects of Time of Day on Job Performance: Evidence from a Day-Level Study.* Journal of Applied Psychology, 100(4), 1045–1055.
- Mackenzie, K., & O'Brien, B. (2018). *The Productivity Project: Accomplishing More by Managing Your Time, Attention, and Energy.* Crown Business.
- Morrison, R. (2020). *Remote Work: An Essential Guide to Work from Home Successfully.* Work-Life Balance Press.
- World Economic Forum. (2020). *The Future of Jobs Report 2020.* Retrieved from World Economic Forum.

CONCLUSION

As we reach the end of this in-depth exploration of the remote work landscape, it is apparent that we stand at the forefront of a new era in professional life. What began as a response to unprecedented global events has evolved into a transformative redefinition of how we view work, collaboration, and professional identities. Remote and hybrid work are no longer temporary solutions but blueprints of a more dynamic, adaptable, and inclusive future.

A Paradigm Shift in the Concept of Work

The shift to remote and hybrid work environments has catalyzed a profound transformation in the very concept of work. It has freed us from traditional constraints, like rigid schedules and physical office spaces, inviting us to explore a model where productivity and flexibility coexist. No longer tied to a desk or a 9-to-5 routine, work has become a more fluid aspect of our lives, intertwined with personal growth, creativity, and self-discovery. This new paradigm asks us to reconsider what it truly means to be productive, to contribute meaningfully, and to maintain a balance between achieving professional goals and honoring personal values.

The Power of Flexibility and Adaptability

In a world that changes faster than ever, the ability to adapt is not merely an asset but a necessity. The COVID-19 pandemic underscored this, showing that those who could pivot quickly, learn new digital tools, and adjust their routines were best positioned to thrive. Flexibility has proven to be the ultimate strength, allowing us to remain resilient in the face of uncertainty and complexity. However, adaptability in this new era goes beyond merely learning new tools; it encompasses a mindset shift, a commitment to continuous learning, and an openness to reinventing our workflows to suit the demands of the moment.

Mastering flexibility requires us to adopt strategies that enhance our capacity for change. Cultivating a growth mindset, honing communication skills, experimenting with diverse routines, and embracing emerging technologies are foundational to success in this new environment. Professionals who can engage with change as an opportunity for growth and improvement will adapt and thrive, setting themselves apart in a world that prizes agility and foresight.

Building Cultures of Trust and Collaboration

Remote work may separate us physically but has also highlighted the importance of connection and trust within teams. Organizations that succeed in this era prioritize psychological safety, enabling individuals to share ideas, voice concerns, and engage openly without fear of judgment. When teams cultivate an environment of trust, collaboration flourishes, and diverse perspectives are celebrated rather than overlooked. This shift from hierarchy to empowerment allows ideas to emerge from every corner of an organization, fueling innovation and ensuring everyone's voice is valued.

Leaders play a pivotal role in fostering this culture. By prioritizing empathy and flexibility, they create a space where team members feel seen, heard, and appreciated. Flexibility becomes a personal attribute and an organizational ethos, shaping a work culture that values results over rigid processes, celebrates diverse work styles, and provides room for experimentation. When teams feel empowered to adapt their workflows, contribute unique ideas, and challenge the status quo, they become engines of creativity, driving the organization toward a more innovative future.

The Evolving Balance of Work and Life

The rise of remote work has redefined the boundaries between our professional and personal lives, challenging us to develop a healthier, more integrated approach to work-life balance. In this new model, work does not detract from life but rather complements it, enabling us to honor personal responsibilities while achieving professional goals. Flexible schedules and the ability to work from various locations have given us the freedom to align our work environments with our individual needs, making space for family, hobbies, and self-care in ways that were previously difficult to achieve.

This integration, however, requires intentionality. Without clear boundaries, remote work can lead to overextension, burnout, and a sense of perpetual work. Professionals must cultivate habits that support well-being, such as setting firm start and end times, taking regular breaks, and engaging in self-care practices like exercise, mindfulness, and outdoor activities. When work becomes part of a well-rounded life rather than the center of it, individuals experience greater satisfaction, reduced stress, and a renewed sense of purpose.

A Broader Talent Landscape and the Promise of Inclusion

Remote work has also broken down geographic barriers, allowing organizations to tap into a global talent pool. By embracing remote and hybrid models, companies can recruit individuals based on talent and expertise rather than location, fostering diversity and broadening perspectives. This shift holds transformative potential for inclusion, enabling people from different backgrounds, time zones, and lifestyles to contribute meaningfully. Diverse teams bring fresh insights, fuel innovation, and drive the organization toward more holistic solutions.

Furthermore, remote work allows organizations to accommodate employees with varying needs related to caregiving responsibilities, physical limitations, or simply the desire for a flexible schedule. This inclusivity extends work benefits to those who may have been previously excluded from traditional office-based roles, contributing to a more equitable and balanced workforce.

The Importance of Communication and Connection

In a remote work setting, communication becomes the glue that holds teams together. Clear, consistent, and empathetic communication prevents misunderstandings, fosters transparency, and ensures everyone remains aligned. Leaders and team members must prioritize active listening, a skill that helps build trust and demonstrates respect for diverse viewpoints. Organizations that invest in practical communication tools—whether through project management platforms, instant messaging apps, or video conferencing—create a virtual environment where collaboration and connectivity are seamless.

Beyond tools, communication requires intentionality. In remote settings, leaders must foster open dialogues, seek input from all team members, and create a culture of feedback and continuous improvement. This approach builds camaraderie and ensures everyone feels part of a cohesive whole, even in a physically dispersed team. When communication is effective, it bridges distances and fosters a shared sense of purpose.

Shaping the Future with Purpose and Curiosity

As we look to the future, we must recognize that the remote work landscape will continue to evolve. Emerging technologies, shifting societal expectations, and the ongoing need for flexibility will reshape how we work and collaborate. Professionals and organizations that commit to lifelong learning, embrace curiosity, and prioritize adaptability will find themselves well-positioned to navigate these changes. Remote work has unlocked new possibilities for growth, fulfillment, and achievement, offering a canvas to redefine success in ways that honor professional aspirations and personal values.

An Invitation to Embrace the Journey Ahead

This new era of work is as much an invitation as a challenge. It invites us to reimagine our careers, teams, and organizations with a sense of agency and purpose. The possibilities for innovation, collaboration, and personal fulfillment are more significant than ever before. However, they require us to engage with change proactively, to be resilient, and to cultivate an openness to the unknown. As we move forward, let us confidently embrace the journey, knowing that adaptability, empathy, and a growth-oriented mindset will serve as our compass.

Remote work has changed where we work and how we live and relate to one another. In a world that prizes flexibility, empathy, and inclusion, we are creating a future that values the individual as much as the team, the process as much as the outcome, and the journey as much as the destination. Together, we can build a work environment that reflects our highest aspirations and paves the way for a new era of achievement, purpose, and well-being.

Looking to the Horizon

In closing, as you navigate this evolving landscape, remember that you are part of a more significant movement redefining the work fabric. Embrace each opportunity for growth, each challenge as a lesson, and each success as a step toward a more fulfilling and balanced life. The future of work is in your hands. With adaptability as your guide, curiosity as your fuel, and purpose as your anchor, you can shape a future that works for you and inspires and uplifts everyone around you.

www.ingramcontent.com/pod-product-compliance
Lightning Source LLC
Chambersburg PA
CBHW071451220526

45472CB00003B/760